SHOCKING

The Surreal World of Elsa Schiaparelli

THE SURREAL WORLD OF
ELSA SCHIAPARELLI

Edited by
Marie-Sophie
Carron de la Carrière

Preface

Some names in the world of fashion have that rare power to evoke an era, a style, or a life as soon as they roll off the tongue or pen. Schiaparelli is unquestionably among them. The legendary photos of the designer by Man Ray and Horst P. Horst come to mind, as does her iconic butterfly print and Wallis Simpson, about to become the Duchess of Windsor, draped in a suggestive lobster dress. Then there are the perfumes with catchy names, witty, whimsical accessories, and collaborations with Jean Cocteau and Salvador Dalí, and all of this against the backdrop of Place Vendôme in Paris. In what ended up being a brief span of time—from the mid-1920s to the beginning of World War II—Elsa Schiaparelli expressed and embodied a moment in the history of French and international fashion. She led a remarkable, independent life as a liberated woman, free to travel and to be inspired, free to create and to emancipate herself from aesthetic codes, first by coming into her own and then by remaining so. She was not one to use the third person, but she concluded her memoirs, *Shocking Life*, published in 1954, with the image of a woman, Schiap, relaxing in Tunisia, lying on a sofa designed by Jean-Michel Frank and lulled by birdsong: "Open the door . . . open the door . . . open the dooor." This dual evocation of her "self" stands forever free, endlessly flirting with the imaginary and the poetic, creating her own worlds, shaped by her Roman humanist roots and her affinity for Parisian surrealism.

The exhibition draws from these surrealist worlds to create the perfect backdrop for a tribute to one of the most important designers of the twentieth century and an innovative pioneer. Nearly 520 works were carefully selected by the curators: Olivier Gabet, director of the Musée des Arts Décoratifs, and Marie-Sophie Carron de la Carrière, head curator of the museum's fashion and textile department. The exhibition was orchestrated by Nathalie Crinière, who has designed several successful exhibitions for our museum in the past. I would like to extend my warmest thanks to each of them. This project, enriched by exceptional loans from museums and collections around the world, would never have seen the light of day without the generous and attentive support of Diego Della Valle, devoted owner of Maison Schiaparelli, and Delphine Bellini, CEO. Thanks to their commitment and that of their artistic director, Daniel Roseberry, the Schiaparelli adventure continues in 2022. Now to open the doors to the stuff dreams are made on.

Johannes Huth
President, Les Art Décoratifs

Elsa Schiaparelli, a Last Dance

Every adjective, catchphrase, hasty sketch, and carefully composed portrait by the world's greatest photographers (with a predilection for May Ray) has been used to describe Elsa Schiaparelli. The pages that follow provide a masterful description of her and offer a new perspective on her work; not an Impressionist landscape composed of many discrete strokes, but a kaleidoscopic panorama, fragments of faces placed next to each other like a collage caught between keepsakes of elegant Victorian engravings and the exquisite corpses of Schiaparelli's surrealist friends. A woman rooted in two centuries, planted firmly between two worlds bordered with Roman palazzi and Louis XIV buildings, she grew up in the shadow of the generous humanism of her father and his family, patiently erudite and brilliant. From this brilliance, Schiaparelli created a life and a celebrated body of work, an achievement not within everyone's reach. When some claimed to be orphans or without a personal history, Schiaparelli investigated her origins and roots, like the flower-child she imagined herself to be, "pagan," to use the name of one of her most beautiful collections. She immersed herself in her past, that of Italy during antiquity and the Renaissance, one forged of revivals, making her approach more akin to that of Aby Warburg, although her name remains linked to another great art historian, Bernard Berenson. Sometimes family trees bear the fruit of happy accidents.

Over a period of some fifteen years, this daughter of an orientalist scholar laid—with rigor and whimsy—the austere foundations of an elaborate grammar and an emancipated vocabulary, recognizable in every respect. Elsa Schiaparelli illustrated with panache the continent's last dance on a volcano during the 1930s. Energetic and creative, she evaded the role of muse, to which so many women are reduced, to concentrate on the essentials: being a client, becoming a designer, never surrendering, being true to herself. She was perceived as full of zest and she knew how to be, she was unconventionally attractive, the very definition of chic for women around the world—Diana Vreeland most of all—but she was also hardworking, visionary, and tender when she spoke of the child she once was and of her loved ones. The last page of her memoirs forever links her to her granddaughters, Marisa and Berry, evoking hands that clasp each other, lifelines blurring together. She could write: her memoirs, *Shocking Life*, published in 1954, are proof of this. She knew how to choose her words to craft compelling hooks and cheeky names for her perfumes. Up to the very end, she wrote about her life, decided how she would be remembered, and how her story would resonate through the history of fashion and art. Just before her death, she chose to donate more than 120 models and 6,000 drawings to the Union Française des Arts du Costume (Ufac), for which the Musée des Arts Décoratifs is responsible and whose collections it has carefully looked after for many years.

After a first retrospective in 2004, a tribute seemed more than ever in order. Not a repeat—that would hardly suit the work, with its infinite stories—but a different focus. As much as Elsa deserves appreciation, Schiaparelli deserves recognition. At a time ripe with discussion about the fertile connections between fashion and art, she would have known how to bring them together joyfully to create precise, irreproachable work. Salvador, Jean, Christian, Jean-Michel, Meret, the other Elsa, Nusch, Leonor, and so many others were her friends, accomplices, elective affinities, partners in crime—their mutual respect was total, their dialogue unfailing. Faced with the abyss of their time, they added color when a field-gray specter was looming on the horizon. The surrealist world supported her as much as she contributed to them: her name and works no longer go forgotten in monographs and specialized books, and anyone who would still dare to omit her would be making a disastrous error.

Links to the past remain intact, true admiration lasts forever: Hubert de Givenchy, Yves Saint Laurent, Sonia Rykiel, Azzedine Alaïa, John Galliano—each appears in the exhibition as a well-deserved tribute. Today the Schiaparelli story continues, in a different way, and with the immensely talented Daniel Roseberry, who, with humility and elegance, expresses the contemporary relevance of what Schiaparelli has represented for nearly a century. She loved to dress women, not to disguise them but to elevate them. She would surely have been proud to see a woman wearing a dress bearing her name on one exceptional day in American history, performing at the president's inauguration.

Everyone knows it, but it bears repeating: an exhibition is a collective endeavor, each one a fresh perspective; an exhibition is an exercise in risk-taking where choices are revealed and defended. Allow me to thank everyone who made *Shocking! The Surrealist World of Elsa Schiaparelli* possible, particularly Marie-Sophie Carron de la Carrière, who curated the exhibition, and Marie-Pierre Ribère for her invaluable help. Thanks also to Nathalie Crinière, who put her talent to work once again, and to the production team, led by Yvon Figueras. My gratitude goes to Dilys Blum, *the* expert on Schiaparelli's work, for her suggestions, and to Valérie Belin, who in selecting certain models from the Ufac and museum Schiaparelli collections, has revealed so much of their magic, details, and prints, like the fleeting rustling of the fabrics. The teams from the fashion and textile and collections departments have once again carried out an exemplary restoration campaign, made possible by the generosity of the Anna Maria and Stephen Kellen Foundation, with the amicable and loyal support of Marina Kellen French, to whom I once again express my great affection. Last but not least, I would like to revisit a conversation with Diego Della Valle and Delphine Bellini that took place one fall evening, when we discussed the possibility of holding an exhibition in the future. It was late 2017. Great things take time: Diego, who acquired and revived Maison Schiaparelli, and Delphine, who supported him with enthusiasm and intelligence, know a little something about that. This exhibition owes much to them, and we extend our warmest thanks to them.

On this occasion, it would be marvelous to conclude with the beginning, the opening words of Schiaparelli's biography: "I merely know Schiap by hearsay. I have only seen her in a mirror. She is, for me, some kind of fifth dimension".

Olivier Gabet
Director, Musée des Arts Décoratifs

ESSAYS

Shocking: Life between the Lines

Marie-Sophie Carron de la Carrière

"Look down, Elsa," he said. I summoned the courage to peer down at the village below, with its central square and the complicated surrounding pattern of twisting, turning streets.

"See, carissima,*" Father said gently. "There is more than one way to the square. Life is like that. If you can't reach your destination by one road, try another."*[1]

A scent of scandal

In November 1954, Elsa Schiaparelli's memoirs, *Shocking Life*, were published in London, New York, and Paris.[2] The cover was fuchsia pink, the couturiere's favorite color, with her signature inscribed across it, while the title played on the double meaning of the word "shocking," both chromatic and moral. That pink was the color adopted by the couturiere in 1937 for the packaging of her perfume Shocking. The fragrance was an opportunity for Schiaparelli to define her conception of a sensational, desirable form of femininity as embodied by the movie star Mae West. The latter, a close friend of Dalí, called upon Schiaparelli to dress her for the cinema. A bust made to her measurements meant the costumes for the American actress could be made in Paris without her having to be present for the fittings. This method of working was adopted for the made-to-measure dresses she wore in *Every Day's a Holiday* (1937), filmed at the Paramount Studios in Hollywood. Schiaparelli collaborated with the surrealist artist Leonor Fini to design the new perfume's bottle, based on the curvaceous lines of Mae West's bared bust, and with the perfumer Jean Carles to determine its olfactory content. The bottle was demurely enshrined, away from prying eyes, in a fuchsia pink box with an air of femininity and glamour. The intense color denoting her heady fragrance was baptized "shocking pink" and became the hallmark of the couturiere, who had by then settled in her new Place Vendôme showrooms. She described its irresistibility in her memoirs: "The colour flashed in front of my eyes. Bright, impossible, impudent, becoming, life-giving, like all the light and the birds and the fish in the world put together, a colour of China and Peru but not of the West—a shocking colour, pure and undiluted."[3] That was how the word came to be the title of her memoirs: "The name had to begin with an 'S', this being one of my superstitions."[4] In addition to denoting the color of the book's cover, the word 'shocking' has a whiff of deliberate provocation about it, to rouse the reader's curiosity.

A divine comedy

Chapter 13 of Schiaparelli's autobiography, recounting her departure from Paris to New York in 1941 in the face of the German Occupation, is introduced with a quotation from *The Divine Comedy* by the late medieval Florentine poet Dante Alighieri that echoed the couturiere's state of mind at that time, beset by doubt.[5] Considered the book of books, the source of Italian literature, the quotation is Schiaparelli's tribute to the great narrative

1. Horst. P. Horst, *Portrait of Elsa Schiaparelli*, gelatin silver print, 1937. Musée des Arts Décoratifs, Paris, gift of the artist, 1994, inv. 993.16.32.

2. Drawings by Christian Bérard reproduced in the French edition of the designer's autobiography, *Shocking, souvenirs d'Elsa Schiaparelli*, 1954.

3. Elsa Schiaparelli photographed at her home, 22 rue de Berri. The photograph was used on the back cover of her autobiography (French edition).

poem. She cites the renowned opening lines of the first canto of *Inferno* where Dante, both character and narrator, actor and spectator, wanders among the heroes of ancient mythology, having found his way out of a dark forest.

> In the middle of the journey of our life
> I came to myself in a dark wood,
> where the straight way was lost.
>
> Ah! how hard a thing it is to tell what a wild,
> and rough, and stubborn wood this was,
> which in my thought renews the fear!
>
> So bitter is it, that scarcely more in death!

This dreamlike vision of a strange and worrying world illuminates the personal journey of Schiaparelli, who was confronted with a similar situation. Her imagination was struck by poem's initiatory narrative, which was both poetic and spiritual, having been introduced to classical Italian literature by her father, an erudite and humanist professor of orientalism.[6] At the age of twenty-one, she published a collection of her own youthful poems titled *Arethusa* with the sub-title *Verba dat omnia Amor* ("Love gives all words").[7] She identified with Arethusa, a nymph from Greek mythology, one of the attendants of Artemis, the goddess of hunting.[8] From a young age, Schiaparelli was irrepressibly drawn to writing which she described as a deeply moving, organic experience: "Then it was that the urge to write came over me. It was like a shock. I felt it from head to foot—so strong that it was practically physical. . . . I wrote for hours on end in a trance. . . . I was possessed. Never since have I experienced such a complete pleasure."[9] Extracts of the lyrical poems written by the solitary young woman, published in a number of Italian newspapers, shocked those close to her with their shameless allusions: "To the family the book came as a bombshell."[10] The weekly *L'Illustrazione italiana* incorrectly referred to Elsa Schiaparelli as the daughter of the renowned astronomer Giovanni, when in fact she was his niece. The article describes a sensitive, stirring collection of the torments of the young poet's soul.[11] The book's dedication illustrates her febrile state, revealing a buried emotion from her childhood or an open wound from her adolescence: "To those I love / To those who love me / To those who have made me suffer."[12] In her memoirs, Schiaparelli refers to the hostile reception accorded to her youthful poems, underlining the profound truths expressed by her juvenile urges and frequent disarray. As she explained: "She knows now. Sorrow, love, ardent sensuality, and mysticism, the heritage of a thousand years, came rushing through the mind of the naïve child. No achievement since has given her such satisfaction."[13] The writer's calling had crossed Schiaparelli's precocious mind, but she renounced it with a witticism: "A writer? Possibly. This was, as I have already pointed out, my first choice, but events led me away from it. Then again so much has been written that there is a little left to say."[14] It is the slow progress from a frustrated writer's calling to an accomplished career as a fashion designer that she recounts to the reader.

In the third person

In her memoirs, Elsa Schiaparelli recounts the exploits of her everyday life in a laconic manner in different temporalities. Sometimes writing in the third person, she refers to herself with the pithy sounding abbreviation of her surname, Schiap, shedding light upon this slightly enigmatic character with gentle irony, as if a double freed from herself, who appears in the very first lines of the book's preface: "I merely know Schiap by hearsay. I've only seen her in a mirror. She is, for me, some kind of fifth dimension."[15] Caught up in the autobiographical game, she gives us a quirky, fragmented interpretation of her, nonetheless delivering a highly constructed text combining dreams and memories of real moments. The spirit of the era unfurls in the background, caught up in the whirlwind of the avant-garde movements of the 1920s and 1930s, notably the surrealist revolution. We encounter lots of people in Schiaparelli's chronicle. The characters—members of her family,

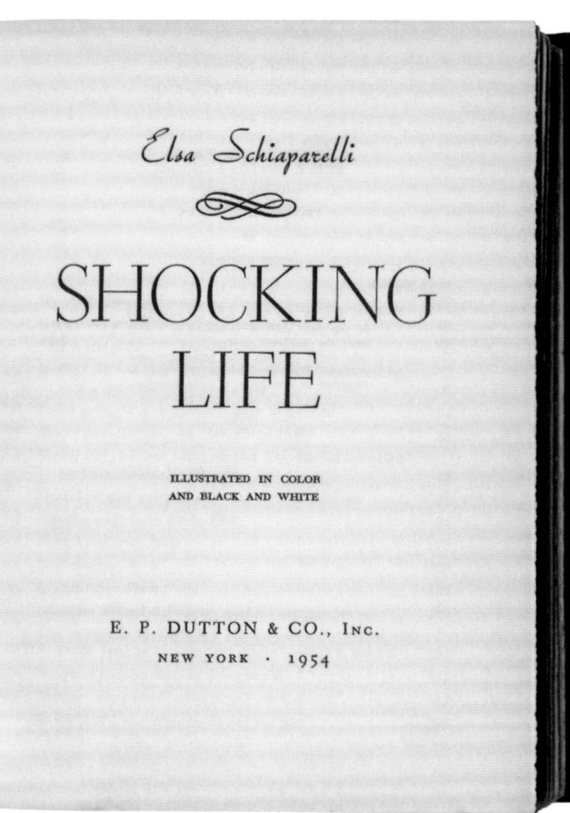

4. Title page of the American edition of Elsa Schiaparelli's autobiography, opposite a reproduction of Pablo Picasso's *Bird Cage and Playing Cards*, oil on canvas, 1937.

5. Jean-Michel Frank's installation in the salon, 21 place Vendôme, photograph, undated. Maison Schiaparelli, Paris.

friends, artists (musicians, painters, writers), and various celebrities—keep coming in a procession from a past era that she analyzes with lucidity in a caustic manner: "She is now of concrete age, but in reality has never grown up. Believing tremendously in friendship, she expects too much of her friends: sheer disappointment in their capacity to respond has often made her enemies."[16]

The French edition is illustrated with sketches by Christian Bérard—seven line drawings of women's heads with hats and fanciful glasses, one of which appears on the title page (ill. 2). One of these hats is a headscarf for the beach in fabric with a newsprint pattern.[17] The couturiere recalls the daring design of the fabric created in 1935 with the textile designer and manufacturer Colcombet: "She clipped newspaper articles about herself, both complimentary and otherwise, in every sort of language, stuck them together like a puzzle, and had them printed on silk and cotton"[18] (see p. 31). Schiaparelli paid tribute to the talent as a fashion illustrator of Bérard, nicknamed Bébé, and to their faithful friendship, with a glowing remark: "To be approved and admired—and sometimes befriended—by Bebe [*sic*] was a consecration in the artistic, social, and intellectual world of Paris."[19] He died in 1949 and was the only artist to illustrate the French edition of Schiaparelli's memoirs. His was also the first name mentioned in a list of those who enchanted her with their creativity: "Working with artists like Bebe [*sic*] Bérard, Jean Cocteau, Salvator Dalí [*sic*], Vertès, Van Dongen; and with photographers like Hoyningen-Hueni [*sic*], Horst, Cecil Beaton, and Man Ray gave one a sense of exhilaration. One felt supported and understood beyond the crude and boring reality of merely making a dress to sell."[20] The back cover of the French edition features a photograph of Schiaparelli at home in 22 rue de Berri, holding a white Bakelite telephone in one hand and her much-loved dog, a shih tzu named Gourou-Gourou, in the other (ill. 3). The realistic portrait evokes the confidential style she used to recount her life, like a long telephone conversation with a friend. The ordinary, domestic image humorously tempers the announcement of the book's shocking content. The same effect was used in the British and American editions, entitled *Shocking Life*. The simultaneous publication of her book in three countries in 1954 was a sign of Schiaparelli's international fame, as well as her attachment to the lifestyles of all three capitals: Paris, London, and New York.

My Picasso

The frontispiece of the American edition of Elsa Schiaparelli's memoirs features a color reproduction of a 1937 Picasso painting, *Birds in a Cage*, that was part of the couturiere's personal collection (ill. 4). The following quotation underlines her unwavering attachment to this painting: "Even though poverty-stricken I wouldn't take a fortune for my Picasso."[21] She describes the painting, which she considered a reflection of her symbolic portrait: "There is a cage. Below it are some playing-cards on a green carpet. Inside the cage a poor, half-smothered white dove looks dejectedly at a brilliantly polished pink apple; outside the cage an angry black bird with flapping wings challenges the sky."[22] For Picasso, it depicted the turmoil of his love life divided between two women, Marie-Thérèse Walter and Dora Maar, here transformed into ferocious birds. In its unsettling approach to reality, the cruel Spanish humor of Picasso's penetrating vision is different from Schiaparelli's perception. Above and beyond the anecdote about the origin of the picture, Schiaparelli admired the capacity of Picasso, a painter of the soul, to reveal the underlying emotions of the human condition. Her sensitive reading of the image echoed her own passionate odyssey. She interpreted it as a representation, both somber and bright, of the feeling of imprisonment linked to the soul's anguish and of liberation upon attaining her ideals. Picasso's picture hung in her Rue de Berri home, complemented by a large, empty, Empire-style birdcage placed on a table.[23] In 1939 *Harper's Bazaar* echoed her taste for collecting old cages.[24] The craze for this new fashion was also taken up by Jean-Michel Frank who installed a Schiaparelli perfume boutique in a birdcage, in Place Vendôme (ill. 5). By way of an epilogue to her memoirs, Schiaparelli describes her living

6. Man Ray, *Elsa Schiaparelli*, gelatin silver print on baryta paper, c. 1934. Musée Cantini, Marseille, acquired in 2019 in remembrance of Monsieur Jean-François Sarnoul, inv. 2019.4.

environment—that of the terrace of her house in Hammamet, Tunisia. Stretched out on a sofa also designed by Jean-Michel Frank, she listens with empathy to the imploring song of a small bird: "Open the door . . . open the door . . . open the dooor [*sic*]."

A family album

Unlike the French edition, the British and American editions of Schiaparelli's memoirs features lots of illustrations. They show the places that were important in her life (Palazzo Corsini in Rome, Place Vendôme in Paris, the garden of her home in Paris, her house in Hammamet, Tunisia). There are also several photographs of her at different ages, ranging from six to sixty-four ("Schiap today"), including the famous surrealist portrait Man Ray took of her in 1934 (ill. 6). Her daughter Gogo and her granddaughters Marisa and Berenthia also feature, as in a family album. The fashion house is documented from different angles by the Dutch photographer Ed van der Elsken: the glazed door opening onto Place Vendôme and the interior of the boutique. The only sartorial creations to be showcased, however, are the trompe l'oeil bow sweater from her first collection, a striped ski mask, and a couture collection that ended on a high note with a wedding dress. A few artists are represented. The most frequent is Christian Bérard, with his line drawings identical to those in the French edition, and some color drawings produced for American *Vogue*, notably the one for the Circus collection. The painter Drian depicted his dear friend in her salon (ill. 8) and was himself photographed in profile with her in front of her fireplace, like a couple of sphynxes facing one another. Marcel Vertès's humorous advertising illustration for depicts a sailor smelling the flowers on the bottle's stopper. Schiaparelli sent herself up by selecting a souvenir photo of a masked ball she attended disguised as a carrot, as well as a press drawing accompanying an imaginary conversation between herself and Stalin, both clad in parachutist outfits in full flight, which appeared in the June 1936 issue of *Vanity Fair* magazine ("Impossible interview"). Memories of trips to Texas, Moscow, and Brazil, with very witty commentaries, complete the visual panorama comprising a patchwork of lively details and picturesque photos.

The golden legend of a couturiere

The Schiaparelli couture house, declared bankrupt, ceased activity on December 13, 1954, the month after the publication of the couturiere's memoirs. Only the fragrance and cosmetics part of the company survived, providing her with a significant source of income. For Schiaparelli, writing her memoirs afforded the opportunity to take stock of her life, from her birth in Rome in 1890 to the closure of her Paris couture house. At the age of sixty-four, she evoked episodes of her accomplished life as a female artist and couture heroine in twenty-one chapters recounted with acerbic wit and an amused eye. She was inspired by her friend and mentor, the couturiere Paul Poiret whom she nicknamed "the Leonardo of fashion."[25] Having read his memoirs with interest, published after the closure of his couture house in 1930, she joked about its choice of title: "Poiret wrote a book called *En habillant la grande époque* [*sic*] (*On Dressing the Grand Era*). It might be better to write a book called *En déshabillant les femmes* (*On Undressing Women*)."[26] Poiret wrote: "There it is in its entirety, this life that lasted fifty years. It fits into one 300-page volume. Should there have been some padding? I'm not upset at having viewed it as a whole and looking at it in an abridged version today."[27] Schiaparelli recounts her youth in detail, as well as her childhood surroundings and the cultural environment that determined her intellectual and artistic education. Barely two years later, Paul Poiret was back with the publication of *Revenez-y* in which he explains: "I didn't say everything because it's impossible to recount fifty years of a life as eventful as mine in a three hundred-page book. . . . I didn't say everything because I limited myself to recounting the most public side of my life, not wishing to touch upon the key chapters of my private life."[28] In her memoirs, Schiaparelli mingles all facets of her life, public and

7. Raoul Dufy, *Fashion Show at Schiaparelli's* (study), c. 1936, gouache on paper. Monaco, Edmond Henrard collection.

private. She polishes her image and offers it up for the admiration of her contemporaries. She points out with flair what sets her apart and makes her matchless. Her sincere, cheerful voice is sometimes overwhelming in its intensity.[29] For her, it was a question of revealing her fate and reviving the myth of the designer as a female artist.

The world according to Elsa Schiaparelli

After writing her memoirs, Schiaparelli dedicated her time, among other things, to assuring her place for posterity in museums in the three cities that had played an important part in her life. She worked on her posthumous recognition with a series of gifts. Firstly, by giving a few of her designs to the Victoria and Albert Museum in London in 1964; then to the Philadelphia Museum of Art in 1969; and lastly, in 1971, to the Union Française des Arts du Costume in Paris, whose collection is overseen by the Musée des Arts Décoratifs.[30] Her writing, completed by these gifts of her most important sartorial creations, constitute the fundamental sources that Elsa Schiaparelli developed to celebrate her imaginative mind and creative energy.

1. Elsa Schiaparelli, "The best advice I ever had," *Reader's Digest*, January 1961, 157.
2. Elsa Schiaparelli, *Shocking Life* (London: J. M. Dent & Sons; E. P. Dutton & Co, New York, 1954). The French title is *Shocking* (Paris: Denoël, 1954).
3. Elsa Schiaparelli, *Shocking Life* (London: J. M. Dent & Sons, 1954), 97.
4. Ibid., 96.
5. Ibid., 137.

8. Étienne Drian, *Madame Schiaparelli in Her Living Room*, undated, oil, gouache, and watercolor on card. Maison Schiaparelli, Paris.

6. Ibid., 3.

7. Elsa Schiaparelli, *Arethusa* (Milan: Riccardo Quintieri, 1911).

8. "Various legends recount Alpheus' attempts to seduce Artemis and the nymphs. Alpheus loved Artemis but the goddess resisted his love, so he decided to capture her by force. . . . Among Artemis' attendants, there was one, Arethusa, whom the god was also in love with. To follow her, he disguised himself as a hunter, like her, and when she fled to the island of Ortygia in Syracuse to escape him, he followed her there. Arethusa was transformed into a stream, but Alpheus mingled with her waters, out of love." Pierre Grimal, *Dictionnaire de la mythologie grecque et romaine* (Paris: Presses Universitaires de France, 1951), 29.

9. Schiaparelli, *Shocking Life*, 20–21.

10. Ibid., 22.

11. Article published in *L'Illustrazione italiana*, July 9, 1911, reproduced in: Marisa Schiaparelli Berenson, *Elsa Schiaparelli's Private Album* (London: Double-Barrelled Books, 2014), 30.

12. "A chi amo / A chi mi ama / A chi mi fece soffrire."

13. Schiaparelli, *Shocking Life*, 21.

14. Ibid., 226.

15. Ibid, ix.

16. Ibid.

17. Schiaparelli, *Shocking Life*, 234.

18. Schiaparelli, *Shocking Life*, 74.

19. Ibid., 76.

20. Ibid., 75.

21. And it continues: "even if, as her mother had once predicted, she should find herself in an empty room with nothing but a crust of bread and straw mattress." Ibid., x.

22. Ibid.

23. Meryle Secrest, *Elsa Schiaparelli: A Biography* (London: Fig Tree, 2014), 327.

24. "Paris collects old bird cages," *Harper's Bazaar*, July 1939, 80–81.

25. Schiaparelli, *Shocking Life*, 43.

26. Ibid., 58.

27. Paul Poiret, *En habillant l'époque* (Paris: Bernard Grasset, 1930), 20.

28. Paul Poiret, *Revenez-y* (Paris: Gallimard, 1932), 7–8.

29. Daniel Roseberry has been the artistic director of Schiaparelli since April 2019. In conversation with Steff Yotka for *Vogue* magazine: "I've never read this book, and I personally have no interest in it either right now. Maybe that's ignorant or wrong, but there is something so overwhelming about her legacy. I feel like the less I know the better. I read a few pages and I was like, 'This is too much. I'm going to be aware of her voice.'" Steff Yotka, "From Bergdorf's to Dover Street Market, Daniel Roseberry Reflects on his Stateside Schiaparelli Takeover," *Vogue*, November 2021.

30. Gifts to the Metropolitan Museum (in 1951): an evening dress and a pair of gloves from her own wardrobe. Gifts to the Victoria and Albert Museum: seven garments. Gifts to the Philadelphia Museum of Art: forty-three garments and seventeen fashion accessories. Gifts to the Union Française des Arts du Costume: 66 garments and 22 fashion accessories, not forgetting 6,387 drawings of her own collections.

Dressing the Modern Woman

Dilys Blum

The selection of Elsa Schiaparelli for the cover of *Time* magazine's August 13, 1934 issue (ill. 1) testified to her growing influence on fashion and the importance of Paris couture to the economies of France and the United States as the two countries emerged from the Great Depression during the 1930s. As the first woman fashion designer to be honored, and only the second to be featured—Jean Philippe Worth appeared on the August 13, 1928 cover—Schiaparelli, muffled in furs, wears a knitted tam perched jauntily on the side of her head. She exudes chic and the "ultra-modern" sensibility that led the weekly magazine to rank her as the "genius" among her contemporaries. *Time* however tempered its praise by suggesting that what prevented Schiaparelli "from becoming the smartest of the Paris dressmakers" was that she was too easily copied. What the writer saw as an obstacle, was in fact one of her greatest strengths. As Schiaparelli later observed in her autobiography *Shocking Life*: "France gave me the inspiration, America the sympathetic approval and the result."[1]

The nearly six years Schiaparelli spent in the United States from 1916 to 1922 played a critical role in the development of her design philosophy and fashion business. She moved to New York with her husband Willie Wendt De Kerlor who was well-known in London psychic and occult circles as a lecturer, writer, and consultant with expertise in palmistry, tarot, clairvoyance, astrology, phrenology, and graphology. As director of the Occult Club in Piccadilly he had a loyal following of mostly titled women and in 1915, a year after his marriage, was unceremoniously deported to France by the British authorities for fortune-telling. The couple met at a talk on theosophy and Schiaparelli was instantly smitten with the charismatic lecturer. Like her favorite uncle, the eminent astronomer Giovanni Schiaparelli, the impressionable twenty-four-year-old was drawn to the "mystic sciences"; her uncle was among the well-known scientists and intellectuals who investigated the claims of the Italian medium Eusapia Palladino in 1892. Elsa and her husband were not alone in their exploration of psychic phenomena and the occult, which during World War I attracted many of the period's modern artists, writers, and intellectuals and later informed surrealism.
Schiaparelli believed much of what she learned during her years with De Kerlor and his impact can be gleaned from his writings and lectures, ranging from "Personal Magnetism: Its Relation to Success" to an "Occult View of Women's Suffrage" to the advertising slogan for his palmistry readings: "KNOW YOURSELF!"—that she adopted as the first of her twelve commandments for women: "Since most women do not know themselves they should try to do so."[2]

During the couple's first two years in New York, De Kerlor translated and edited two works by Émile Boirac, a French philosopher and parapsychologist, who along with Schiaparelli's uncle, had scrutinized Palladino's claims. The first book, *La Psychologie inconnue* (*Our Hidden Forces*), was published in 1917. The second, *L'Avenir des sciences psychiques* (*The Psychology of the Future*), published in 1918, includes photographs of Schiaparelli participating in several psychic experiments. Her dress flirts with design ideas that would later become signature details in her couture collections, from the surplice top adapted from the Japanese kimono, the dramatic sculpted belt buckle, to sensibly styled footwear (ill. 2). The most distinguishing feature, however, is her hair, cut into a fashionable Joan of Arc bob popularized in 1916 by Gabrielle Chanel. Schiaparelli's "unkempt" version reflects the bohemian influences of Greenwich Village where the couple lived in hotels as boarders and identifies her as a modern, independent

1. Cover of *Time*, August 13, 1934.

FIFTEEN CENTS (IN CANADA, 20c Reason: Tariff) August 13, 1934

TIME

The Weekly Newsmagazine

Stevens Rockwell—Paris

Volume XXIV

MME ELSA SCHIAPARELLI

. . . glorifies the gadget, persecutes the button.

(See BUSINESS)

Number 7

Circulation Office, *350 East 22nd Street, Chicago.* (Reg. U. S. Pat. Off.) Editorial and Advertising Offices, *135 East 42nd Street, New York.*

woman. It contrasts with the sleek sophisticated look she later adopted in Paris where she was coiffed by the celebrated hair stylist Antoine.

Following her estrangement from De Kerlor after the birth of their daughter in June 1920, she found allies in women in similar circumstances. Her developing friendships with Gabrielle Buffet-Picabia and Blanche Hays were a lifeline both emotionally and financially and opened new possibilities. Buffet-Picabia, who was separated from the French artist Francis Picabia, introduced Schiaparelli to New York's modern art scene through the Société Anonyme recently founded by Katherine Dreier, Marcel Duchamp, and Man Ray. Schiaparelli assisted with office work for the society's inaugural exhibition in 1920 and surely found a spiritual meeting of minds in Dreier who was an ardent Theosophist. At the same time Buffet-Picabia introduced Schiaparelli to Paris couture. As the American agent for couturiere Nicole Groult, sister of Paul Poiret, she enlisted Schiaparelli's help in selling Groult's designs in New York. Although the venture was a failure, it provided a valuable lesson in American taste and buying habits. In Paris, Buffet-Picabia introduced her to Paul Poiret[3] whose reputation as the King of Fashion had been overshadowed by Gabrielle Chanel. Poiret generously mentored Schiaparelli who was searching for a style of her own and provided her with the latest designs to wear out on the town. Their shared sensibility was evident years earlier in the impromptu evening ensemble

2. Elsa Schiaparelli practicing spiritism, photograph reproduced in Émile Boirac, *The Psychology of the Future*, 1918, p. 49.

Schiaparelli designed for a ball she attended on her first visit to Paris around 1911. The style echoed Poiret's revolutionary harem pants ensemble then in fashion and at the same time, recalled images of "Orientalist" dress she likely encountered in the Lincei Library[4] where her father, a specialist in Arabic languages, was librarian or in his private library that she described as "my haven and joy."[5] Schiaparelli's version was created from 4 yards of dark blue crepe de chine purchased at the Galeries Lafayette that she wrapped between her legs for a baggy effect and pinned it in place. Complemented by an orange silk sash and turban created from an additional 2 yards of silk, the ensemble hinted at the dramatic and unconventional color combinations that would become a Schiaparelli signature.

When Schiaparelli took up Blanche Hays offer to share an apartment in Paris with their daughters, it provided her with the ideal opportunity for reinvention. Hays, recently separated from the renowned American lawyer Arthur Garfield Hays, was a costume designer and actress with the Greenwich Village avant-garde theater company Provincetown Players when she and Schiaparelli met in New York. In Paris, Hays introduced Schiaparelli to her American friend Edna Hartley, another single woman who left New York with her daughter, with the intention of becoming a costume designer for the stage or a fashion journalist. Instead, she acquired a small couture house Maison Lambal and in 1926 invited Schiaparelli to design a small collection of sports, day, and evening ensembles. The American trade paper *Women's Wear Daily* singled out the unidentified couturiere for designs that were "carefully conceived" with "individuality and interest."[6]

Modernity in black and white

The closure of the house, precipitated by Hartley's marriage to textile manufacturer Pierre Benedictus, provided Schiaparelli with the impetus to establish her own business in 1927. She began selling hand-knitted sweaters with modernist patterns made by a group of Armenian women from her apartment at 20 rue de l'Université. The tweed-like effect produced using a traditional Armenian knitting stitch and two different colors of yarn ensured that the sweaters kept their shape unlike others on the market. The trompe l'oeil bow design in black and white (ill. 3) was an instant hit and attracted the interest of an American sportswear manufacturer who was importing avant-garde designs by Sonia Delaunay and Erté. The sweater's unprecedented success prompted Charles Kahn, a director of Galeries Lafayette, originally founded by his brother Alphonse and cousin Théophile Bader, to invest in Schiaparelli's business as equal partners. This allowed her to move to the more fashionable 4 rue de la Paix where she remained until 1935. The bow sweater quickly entered the fashion lexicon as a symbol of modernity; machine-knitted versions manufactured in the United States and Austria in all price ranges and color combinations filled department store windows and was published as a knitting pattern in a popular American women's magazine without Schiaparelli's name. The extraordinary success of her sweaters gave birth to the rags-to-riches myth—which Schiaparelli did little to correct during the 1930s—of an impoverished young single mother who became an international sensation during the Great Depression with the only tools she had available: knitting needles. Singled out as a role model for modern women, she was profiled in numerous books offering business advice as an example of what could be achieved from humble beginnings and hard work.

The modern Schiaparelli look during the late 1920s and early 1930s was defined by black and white. She adopted the combination not only for her own dress, but for her salon and home decorated by Jean-Michel Frank, whose vision she continued to champion throughout the 1930s. The most modern of women wore Schiaparelli's black and white designs. For modiste Madame Agnès, patron of Jean Dunand, the stark palette was in perfect harmony with her black and white hair, leading *Harper's Bazaar* to comment in 1930 that "she looked like a modern mantlepiece ornament in black and white china."[7] For a *jolie laide* like Marie-Laure, Vicomtesse de Noailles, who with her husband Charles, the foremost patrons of modern art and architecture in France, black and white was the perfect foil for the sophisticated unconventional looking woman with a strong profile and irregular features, whose elegance was distinguished by angles rather than curves.

Schiaparelli, like her mentor Poiret, believed that architecture was the basis of all art, that fashion was art, and the couturiere an artist. As the American art critic Helen Appleton Read observed in 1931: "Schiaparelli is modern in the real sense of the word. Modern, as for example, the architects Le Corbusier and Mies van der Rohe are in the houses they build, in that her effort is to get back to the fundamental principles. She designs clothes which shall express the original concept of clothes translated into the special needs and tastes of today. Being an artist, this very functionalistic principle, to borrow a term from the architects, is never merely utilitarian, but has beauty of design and proportion. It is real modern as opposed to the rather widespread misconception of the term which assumes modern means bizarre and ultra."[8] Janet Flanner in 1932 further observed that it was "the un-European modernity of her silhouettes, their special applicability to a background of square shouldered skyscrapers, of mechanics in private life, and pastimes devoted to gadgetry"[9] that contributed to her success in the United States.

Schiaparelli's sports clothes, designed for the fashionable active woman or spectator, ranged from divided skirts for playing golf or tennis (ill. 4) to beach pajamas to ski outfits and for the woman pilot who flew her own plane, a complete wardrobe including a comfortable flight suit and an evening gown. Her designs reframed fashion for the modern age believing that the well-toned body gave structure to the silhouette: "Never fit the dress to the body, but train the body to fit the dress."[10]

By 1929 sports clothes were falling out of favor and fewer models were included in the Paris collections. Marjorie Howard of *Harper's Bazaar* attributed this to designs becoming formulaic and offering limited opportunities for couturieres to express "invention and imagination."[11] By 1932 Schiaparelli had strategically expanded her business from "Pour le sport" to "Pour la ville"—"Pour le soir." Her success could be measured in the four

3. Elsa Schiaparelli, trompe l'oeil sweater, 1927. Philadelphie, Philadelphia Museum of Art, 1969, don Elsa Schiaparelli, 1969, inv. 1969-232-54.

4. Elsa Schiaparelli in Hyde Park, London, wearing culottes, unknown photographer, May 19, 1931.

hundred employees who turned out seven to eight thousand garments in eight ateliers each season. Schiaparelli's inventive silhouettes spoke to the times with their extended shoulders and aerodynamic silhouettes, such as the evening gown worn by Arlette Marchal in the film *La Femme idéale* in 1934 (ill. 5). Metal clips replaced buttons and colorful plastic zippers worn on the outside substituted for hidden fastenings. Often chic was in the fabric—rayon was woven to look like tree bark while the new Rhodophane was as transparent as glass. Schiaparelli was the mother of invention and every fashion editor marveled at the wealth of ideas she presented each season. With the purchase of one model garment manufacturers could extract dozens of ideas for new designs.

In line with readers' tastes

As she learned from De Kerlor, the key to success was "personal magnetism." From the beginning Schiaparelli focused on making herself a household name. During the early 1930s, advertisements paired her photograph and distinctive signature in endorsements for American-made fabrics, stockings, and shoes that she used in her Paris collections as a cost-cutting enticement to manufacturers who would be reproducing her models in the United States. Throughout her career she courted visibility particularly with the American press whose extensive coverage of her many personal and business trips, interviews, and lectures were usually prefaced by one of her more controversial comments on the state of fashion design in Paris versus New York. During the 1930s, Schiaparelli's biggest market continued to be the

13e Année. No 1523. 16 pages. — 30 centimes - n° 279 - 18-8-34.

LE FILM COMPLET DU SAMEDI

LA FEMME IDÉALE

avec René Lefèvre et Arlette Marchal

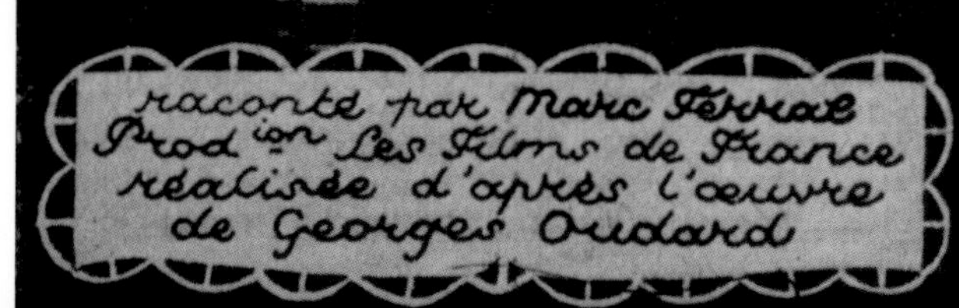

Voir, page 16, notre page illustrée: CINÉ-REVUE

United States where her clothes were copied directly or modified for the wider market. The Schiaparelli look featured in the elite fashion magazines, filtered down to the mass market. Photographs of American, British, and French socialites by Man Ray, Hoyningen-Huene, Horst, and Cecil Beaton for *Vogue* and *Harper's Bazaar* were translated into line drawings for the popular women's magazines[12] in the United States and Europe whose readers were young women who "dare to be different"[13] and housewives and mothers who brought up their own children, did their own cooking, and sewed their own clothes or could turn to the dressmaker around the corner. The fashion illustrations streamlined the most fashion forward elements of Schiaparelli's "hard chic" look and toned down her silhouettes, so they were more acceptable to the magazine's readers and easily reproduced using inexpensive home-sewing patterns available through mail order. Her collections were according to British fashion editor Allison Settle "the perfect expression of the ideas of her age."[14] No matter her income, the modern woman could be beautifully turned out in some version of Schiaparelli's exquisitely tailored coats and suits or for an evening out in the couturiere's signature dinner ensemble with its embellished jacket.

In 1935 Schiaparelli relocated her couture salon to 21 place Vêndome and added the Schiap Shop, a boutique that offered everything from scarves to costume jewelry to be taken away for immediate enjoyment. The first collection, Stop, Look, and Listen, presented in January for summer 1935, declared that the Schiaparelli woman had finally come of age. It celebrated her international reputation in fabrics printed with a collage of her press clippings from American, English, Swedish, German, and French newspapers (ills. 6 and 7). She was no longer an abstraction built on modernist design principles but was now fully connected to the wider world of current events, economics, politics, history, and art. In her memoirs, Bettina Ballard, former fashion editor for American *Vogue* wistfully reflected on Schiaparelli's influence: "There are still many women who yearn for the confidence that her clothes gave them. A Schiaparelli customer did not have to worry as to whether she was beautiful or not she was a type. She was noticed wherever she went, protected by an armor of amusing conversation smartness. Her clothes belong to Schiaparelli more than they belonged to her—it was like borrowing someone else's chic, and, along with it, their assurance."[15]

5. *La Femme idéale* (*An Ideal Woman*), dir. André Berthomieu, 1934, on the cover of the magazine *Le Film complet du samedi*.

6. Josephine Baker, holding a Schiaparelli silk scarf, arrives in Manhattan aboard the *Normandie*, 1935.

1 Elsa Schiaparelli, *Shocking Life* (London: J. M. Dent & Sons, 1954), 122.

2. Schiaparelli, *Shocking Life*, 230.

3. Buffet-Picabia introduced Man Ray to Poiret around 1924.

4. The library of the Accademia Nazionale dei Lincei, one of the oldest and most prestigious scientific institutions in Europe, is located in the Palazzo Corsini in Rome. As a child, Elsa Schiaparelli lived with her parents in an apartment in the building.

5. Schiaparelli, *Shocking Life*, 3.

6. "Both Tussore Frock and Wool Jumper in Sports Ensemble by Lambal," *Women's Wear Daily*, March 30, 1926, 3, 38.

7. *Harper's Bazaar*, June 1930, 138.

8. Helen Appleton Read, "Simplifies Fashion-Wins Fame," *The Brooklyn Daily Eagle*, September 20, 1931, 85.

9. Janet Flanner, "Profiles: Comet," *New Yorker*, June 18, 1932, 19.

10. Number ten of the Twelve Commandments for Women.

11. Marjorie Howard, "High Lights on the Paris Collections," *Harper's Bazar*, April 1929, 88.

12. Sewing patterns featuring adaptations and reproductions of Schiaparelli's designs were pulished in *McCall's*, *Ladies' Home Journal*, and Pictorial Review magazines in particular. The Paris Pattern Company's authentic reproductions of original designs illustrated in *Ladies' Home Journal* were also available in some stores. After World War II, Vogue Patterns offered a new series, the Vogue Paris Original Models.

13. Schiaparelli, *Shocking Life*, 230; number five of the Twelve Commandments for Women.

14. Alison Settle, *Clothes Line* (London: Methuen, 1937), 14.

15. Bettina Ballard, *In My Fashion* (London: Secker & Warburg, 1960), 71.

7. Elsa Schiaparelli, silk scarf, 1935. Philadelphia Museum of Art, Philadelphia, inv. 2020-8-1, purchased with the Costume and Textiles Revolving Fund, 2020.
The print, by Colcombet, features a collage of Elsa Schiaparelli press clippings from American, English, Swedish, German, and French newspapers.

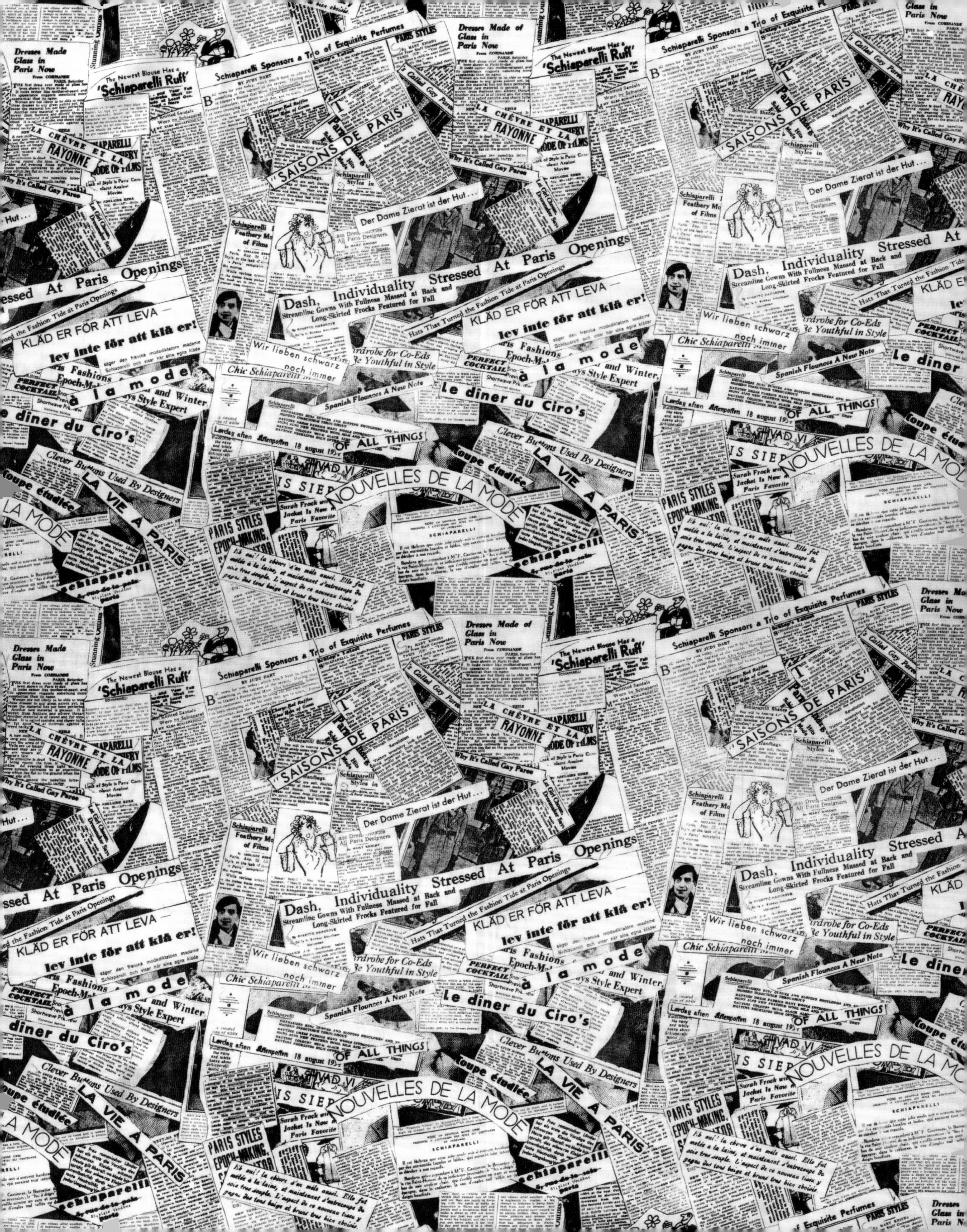

Dresses Made of Glass in Paris Now
The Newest Blouse Has a 'Schiaparelli Ruff'
Schiaparelli Sponsors a Trio of Exquisite Perfumes
BY JUDY DART
PARIS STYLES
"SAISONS DE PARIS"
LA CHÈVRE ET LA RAYONNE
Why It's Called Gay Paree
Der Dame Zierat ist der Hut...
Schiaparelli Feathery Mode of Films
Dash, Individuality Stressed At Paris Openings
Streamline Gowns With Fullness Massed at Back and Long-Skirted Frocks Featured for Fall
Hats That Turned the Fashion Tide at Paris Openings
KLÄD ER FÖR ATT LEVA —
lev inte för att klä er!
Wir lieben schwarz noch immer
Wardrobe for Co-Eds Be Youthful in Style
Chic Schiaparelli
PERFECT COCKTAIL
à la mode
Spanish Flounces A New Note
le diner du Ciro's
Lørdag aften Aftenposten 18 august
"OF ALL THINGS"
Clever Buttons Used By Designers
coupe étudiée
NOUVELLES DE LA MODE
LA VIE A PARIS
Surah Frock with Jacket Is Now Paris Favorite
PARIS STYLES EPOCH-MAKING
SCHIAPARELLI
Eh oui! la chèvre s'est mêlée aussi. Elle fut mêlée à la laine, et maintenant s'entrecoupe de soie très souple. L'aspect de ce nouveau tissu y gagne. Des tons beige et brun très bien choisis
schiaparelli

Man Ray and Elsa Schiaparelli: *Fair Weather* for Creativity

Emmanuelle de l'Écotais

The two creative giants Man Ray and Elsa Schiaparelli have many things in common. Let's start with the most obvious: they were both born in 1890 and both chose Paris after first visiting the city at about the same time—in July 1921 for Man Ray and in June 1922 for Schiaparelli. Both launched themselves in the world of fashion thanks to the encouragement of Paul Poiret, the most successful fashion designer of the time.[1]

However, although Man Ray photographed Schiaparelli and her creations many times in the early 1930s, they apparently did not develop close ties and there is no proven, official collaboration between the two. Schiaparelli never commissioned Man Ray for her collections as she did with Salvador Dalí, Jean Dunand, and Jean Cocteau. Nor did she ask him to photograph her collections: magazines, and especially their art directors (such as Alexey Brodovitch at *Harper's Bazaar*), commissioned images from the photographer. On the other hand, in terms of portraits of herself in which she almost always wore her own creations, we can imagine that she chose her photographer with care. Believing herself "ugly,"[2] the challenge for her was enormous: the photograph, like the clothes, had to bring out "the secret loveliness of women considered plain."[3]

In his autobiography,[4] Man Ray mentions that he met Schiaparelli for the first time in New York in 1919. They knew each other through Gabriële Buffet-Picabia. The two women had met in 1916 on the *Chicago*, the ocean liner that brought them to North America. Gabriële was joining her husband Francis Picabia, a Dada artist and close friend of Marcel Duchamp. Each woman was going through the torment of a chaotic marriage, they thus became inseparable and Gabriële introduced Elsa to all her New York friends, including Man Ray. He had just founded, with Marcel Duchamp and Katherine Dreier,[5] the Société Anonyme, Inc., a contemporary art museum in the Dada spirit. In parallel to his own art, he photographed artists and writers, and had just won a prize for his portrait of the young artist Berenice Abbott.[6] "Another young woman came in from time to time; it was Elsa Schiaparelli, whom I also photographed but not so successfully. She was exotic-looking,[7] Italian and related to a famous astronomer. She was unhappy, separated from her husband, and looking for something to do. She soon left for France with some knitting that was different from the usual sort of thing, and became the well-known couturiere. Years later in Paris I had the satisfaction of doing her portrait which was a triumph."[8] Unfortunately, nothing remains of the sessions when Schiaparelli posed for him in New York.

Surprisingly, and despite the significant number of portraits Man Ray later took of Schiaparelli (over twenty if we count the variations in each series) and his photographs of her collections published during the 1930s in *Harper's Bazaar* (sixteen in all compared with six for Chanel, five for Alix, and two for Lanvin), he didn't write anything else about her in his *Self-Portrait*.[9]

In the same way, Elsa Schiaparelli wrote almost nothing about Man Ray in *Shocking Life*.[10] She hardly mentioned his name alongside the many other personalities of the time she cited: "Working with artists like Bebe [*sic*] Bérard, Jean Cocteau, Salvador Dalí, Vertès, Van Dongen; and with photographers like Hoyningen-Hueni [*sic*], Horst, Cecil Beaton, and Man

1. Man Ray, *Elsa Schiaparelli*, silver gelatin negative, c. 1931. Musée National d'Art Moderne – Centre de Création Industrielle, Paris, gift of M. Lucien Treillard, 1995, inv. AM 1995-281 (1398).

Ray gave one a sense of exhilaration. One felt supported and understood beyond the crude and boring reality of merely making a dress to sell."[11] Further along, Man Ray's name was associated with Jean Cocteau: "Jean Cocteau made some drawings of heads for me. I reproduced some of these on the back of an evening coat, and one, with long yellow hair reaching to the waist, on a grey linen suit. I used to see him often. He had already tried his hand in the film world with the surrealist Death of a Poet [*sic*].[12] Man Ray was the photographer."[13]

But there was no doubt that during their meetings in New York, Schiaparelli must have discussed her memories of Paris with Man Ray. She had already spent a few months in the City of Lights, which both attracted and inspired avant-garde artists, and it is possible that her experience helped convince Man Ray to move there.

His first portrait of Schiaparelli appeared fairly late, on September 27, 1931, in *La Femme de France* (ill. 1): "Madame Schiaparelli, photographed by the artist Man Ray, dressed in one of her charming creations: a dress with long, fan-shaped pleats and a rooster-feather collar,"[14] a trompe l'oeil in the style of ancient Greek pleating produced in collaboration with Jean Dunand. However, her early collections, featured in *Vogue* beginning in 1927, were not photographed by Man Ray—who was taking portraits of elegant Parisian women for the magazine at the time—but by Baron George Hoyningen-Huene,[15] a German fashion photographer prolific during the 1920s and 1930s. These photographs, with their classic beauty, did not convey Schiaparelli's modernism and originality. We can easily imagine that as soon as she could, and especially for her portrait, she chose a photographer who could create an image that would evoke her strong character and avant-garde vision.

As Schiaparelli saw it, Man Ray seemed to be part of the vast nebulous surrealist group she wanted to be part of. It must be said that, as soon as he arrived in Paris, Man Ray became the official photographer of the Dada movement and then the surrealists, creating works that André Breton himself considered the most representative and emblematic of the movement. These included *Voici le domaine de Rrose Sélavy* (1920), published by Man Ray in 1922 in *Littérature* magazine.[16] This work, later known under the name *Dust Breeding*, was a photographic illusion that tried to pass off a reproduction of an artwork (Marcel Duchamp's *Large Glass with Dust Motes*[17]) as an aerial photo of an unreal "dry and fertile" field. Meanwhile, black and white trompe l'oeil was precisely what Elsa Schiaparelli chose to accent in her imaginary bow on the sweaters that marked her first success in 1927.

Let's look at three artworks: in around 1930, Man Ray, in keeping with the Comte de Lautréamont's precept—"as handsome . . . as the chance juxtaposition of a sewing machine and an umbrella on a dissecting table"[18]—took a photo of a lobster placed on the stomach of an classical bust of a woman with no arms or head (ill. 2). Three years later, Minotaure published a spectacular portrait of Elsa Schiaparelli by Man Ray showing her face surrounded by sculpted hair emerging from the same statue (ill. 3). Finally in 1937, Schiaparelli's summer haute couture collection included the renowned evening gown with lobster motif, officially the result of her collaboration with Dalí (see p. 47). The same erotic charge appears for both the dress and Man Ray's first photo, but neither he or she ever mentioned collaborating on it.

Examples of this type multiplied over the years: Man Ray's photographs of butterflies—in black and white (see p. 96), but also in color, worth noting as it was rare in his work at the time—seem to have inspired her summer 1937 collection. The butterfly is one of the animals of which the surrealists (and Schiaparelli) were particularly fond; they saw in them the idea that even ugliness can be transformed into beauty. The insects (beetles, flies, and cicadas) Man Ray photographed in the 1920s are also found on a fascinating necklace from Schiaparelli's fall 1938 collection or on her Pagan collection jacket (see p. 117) whose collar is embellished with insect jewelry. In 1933, during his vacation in Cadaqués with Dalí, Man Ray photographed the artist with his head upside down and a shoe resting on his chin.

A few years later for the winter 1937–38 collection, Schiaparelli designed a shoe hat in collaboration with Dalí. In 1935 Man Ray photographed

2. Man Ray, *Lobster*, silver gelatin negative, c. 1930. Paris, Musée National d'Art Moderne – Centre de Création Industrielle, payment in kind 1994, inv. AM 1994-393 (2466).

hands painted by Picasso (see p. 84); Schiaparelli's winter 1936–37 collection included suede gloves with painted nails. The long blond hair embroidered on the sleeve of an evening jacket in her fall 1937 collection closely resembled a Man Ray photo from 1926,[19] although the jacket was officially made in collaboration with Jean Cocteau (see p. 59). Schiaparelli's successive perfume bottle shapes clearly call to mind works by Man Ray: the truncated bust of Shocking, although inspired by Mae West's figure, echoes the classical bust mentioned above and also Man Ray's photographs of blouses for *Harper's Bazaar*; the pipe she chose as the container for Snuff perfume in 1939 is a literal citation of Man Ray's *Ce qui manque à nous tous* (1927). Sleeping, the Schiaparelli scent introduced in the summer of 1940, identically reproduces the harlequin head in Man Ray's *Fair Weather* from fall of 1939.

It is precisely this head that indicates that the figure was a self-portrait Man Ray's painting, described two years earlier by André Breton as "the man with a magic-lantern head."[20] However, it is possible, as Dilys Blum believes,[21] that the opposite is true: that the evening coat from Schiaparelli's spring 1939 Commedia dell'arte collection inspired the outfit worn by Man Ray's figure. But according to Man Ray, he saw these faces in his dreams: "I . . . turned to painting, executing several large canvases. One of these was a composition of several dreams, done in brilliant colors and using all techniques, from Impressionist to Cubist and Surrealist. . . . One night I heard distant guns, and when I fell asleep again, dreamed that two mythological animals were at each other's throats on my roof. I made a sketch of this and incorporate it in the dream painting, which I called: *Le Beau Temps* (Fair Weather)."[22]

Schiaparelli probably borrowed some of Man Ray's more striking subjects unconsciously since they shared the Dadaist taste for provocation. Repurposing objects was a regular practice for these artists, especially Man Ray who in 1919 originally titled his photograph of an eggbeater

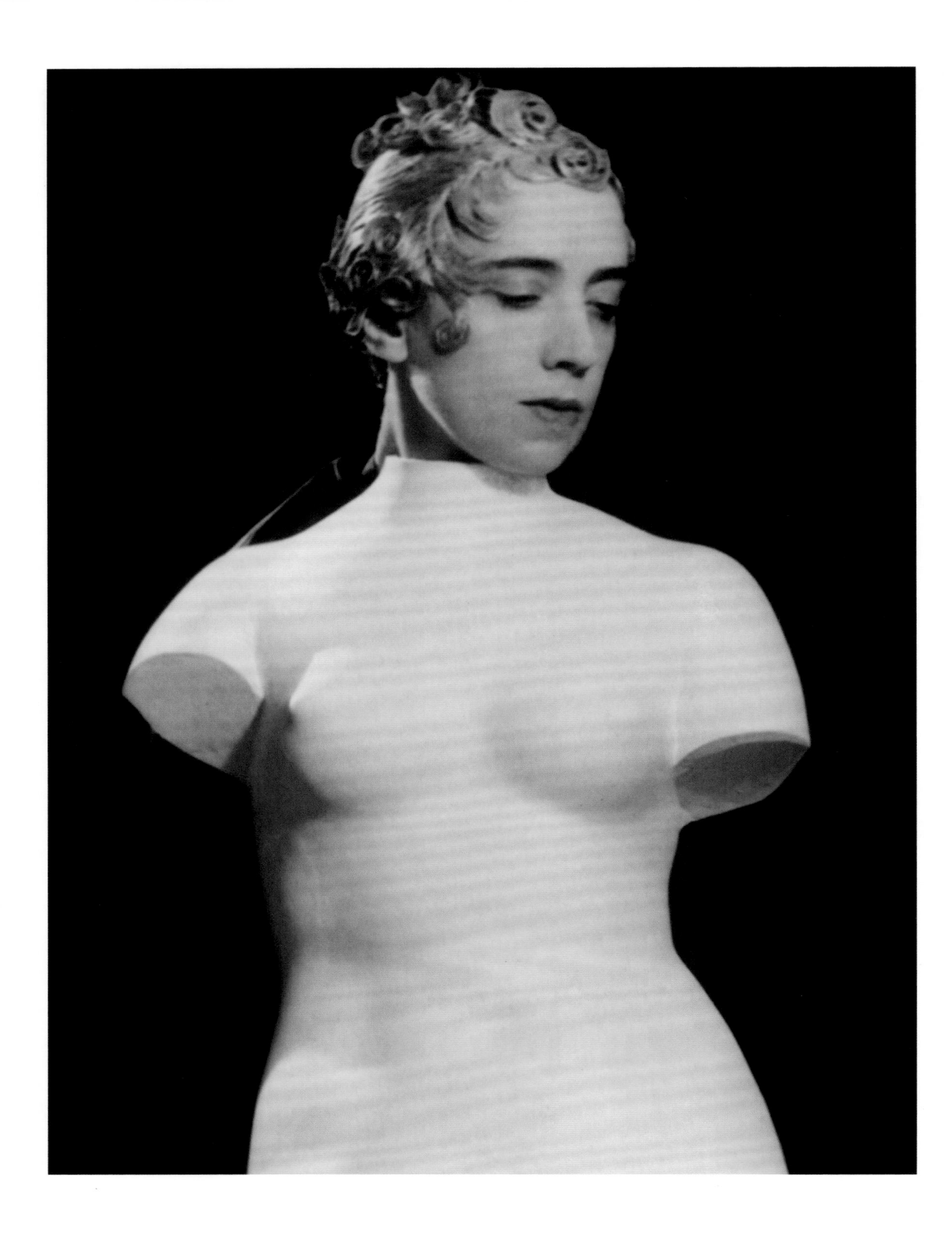

3. Man Ray, *Untitled*, gelatin silver print, c. 1933. San Francisco, San Francisco Museum of Modern Art, The Helen Crocker Russell and William H. and Ethel W. Crocker Family Funds purchase.

4. Tristan Tzara, "D'un certain automatisme du gout," photographs by Man Ray, *Minotaure*, December 1933, nos. 3-4, p. 83.

Man—risqué humor Schiaparelli would certainly have appreciated since she had written erotic poems and designed accessories that were extremely suggestive. Thus, three of her hats illustrating an essay by Tristan Tzara entitled "D'un certain automatisme du gout" appeared in *Minotaure* with Man Ray's photographs[23] (ill. 4). Though Elsa Schiaparelli was not named, we recognize her famous "mad cap."[24] Her hats were shown as examples to illustrate the "emphasis on different parts of the anatomy for which the adornments serve at once as *sign* and *summons*,"[25] unconsciously motivated by the libido. Thus, "The hats women recently still wore; hats with creased crowns folded into a slit, which at first must have imitated those for men; hats whose resemblance, in the course of their evolution, to a woman's genitals, has become not only striking but significant on several grounds; these finally confirm in spectacular fashion what I am suggesting through two characteristic examples: the hat executed in garter elastic and the one whose crown is surrounded by a garnish imitating a detachable collar with

sérieux correctif ou agirait comme acte de compensation. Ou serait-ce là la représentation idéalisée des pouvoirs d'accessibilité au sexe, représentation parallèle au fonctionnement mental ayant sa racine dans les refoulement, les interdictions, surmontées ou non, du sujet ? Qu'on s'imagine ce qui peut déterminer, parmi des dizaines de modèles, le choix d'un chapeau plutôt que d'un autre. Il correspond infailliblement à un désir humain précis de la femme et à travers les hésitations et les flottements, la loi esthétique qu'elle s'est créée se transformera en prétexte et médiateur nécessaire, bientôt systématisé au point de devenir automatique. Dans la série de chapeaux fendus, selon leur degré d'ouverture, on trouve soit la pureté imagée et schématisée, pour ainsi dire idéalement sculpturale des sexes de femme, soit le froissé des chairs meurtries (voir les chapeaux de deuil, où la représentation des sexes douloureux et noirs, morts, pendant en lambeaux jusqu'aux déchirures de chair pour rejoindre la désolation et la souffrance et répondant à des désirs masochistes de douleurs affichées) ou de simulacre de renversement complet, où le contenu de la fente, au lieu d'indiquer le vide, est entièrement retourné par rapport à la surface visible, (caractère anal). Certains de ces couvre-chefs s'ornent de boutons, de rubans, de *scarifications* (remarquables), d'indications de cousu en tant que possibilité d'augmenter ou de réduire à volonté la largeur de la fente (c'est-à-dire les lacets n'étant pas tirés jusqu'à faire se joindre les bords des valves), d'anneaux métalliques passés à travers les lèvres, ô involontaire chasteté, d'une masse avec couleurs pâles et opalescentes, à motifs décoratifs à peine indiqués, de substance visqueuse, coagulée et translucide, évoquant vaguement des plantes, des fruits et des fleurs, débordant les bords de la fente comme si elle s'écoulait de l'intérieur.

MAN RAY

Au cours de mon enquête, il me fut donné d'observer qu'une réelle opposition était présentée dans certains cas quant à la possibilité même de suivre cette mode. Quoique les raisons invoquées fussent toujours de l'ordre du goût et de l'esthétique, il est indéniable que les déterminantes de ceux-ci sont à chercher dans des inhibitions simples, le plus souvent le refus d'envisager sous une forme publique la vie sexuelle. Les chapeaux à large ouverture étant les plus difficile à porter, je tiens les renseignements d'un grand magasin, sont les meilleur marché (à condition égale de matériel et de travail). Il faut conclure que le nombre de femmes à représentation vaginale large est le plus réduit. Mon expérience personnelle m'apprit, par contre, que des femmes très refoulées sous ce rapport portaient aussi des chapeaux à grande ouverture ; l'explication est à chercher dans une identité, sur un plan donné, des contraires qui se joignent apparemment.

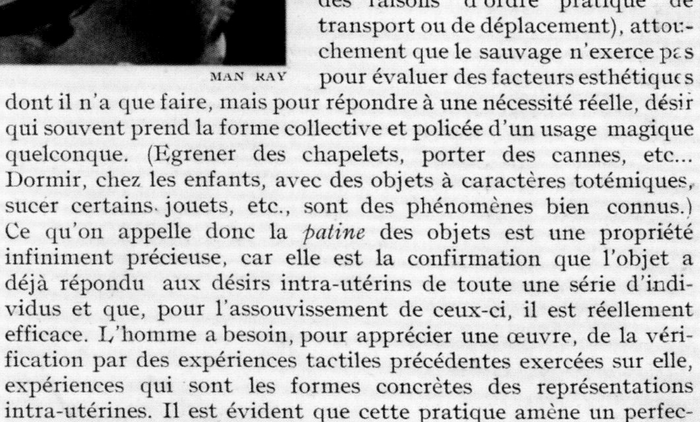

MAN RAY

Ce qui me semble résulter de ce rapide compte-rendu est que, indépendamment de la mode du moment — cette question intéressant particulièrement les lois économiques et l'alternance des symbolismes sexuels masculins et féminins, — la femme placée devant la nécessité du *choix* se réfugie dans des considérations inventées pour masquer ses mobiles intimes (désirs intra-utérins, exhibitionnisme des facultés érotiques, etc.), dans une théorie du goût et de l'esthétique qu'elle se fabrique inconsciemment mais avec ingéniosité à cette intention. Qu'une femme ne se trompe jamais dans ses goûts, veut dire uniquement que les déterminantes de sa sexualité trouvent toujours leur expression, la plus directe et sincère dans l'objet de son choix de vêtements et d'ornements. L'automatisme du goût agit chez elle en dehors de toute raison et la transformation des désirs en symboles existants, au moyen du transfert, s'opère avec une suprême habileté.

Que l'esthétique n'ait pas une existence de lois propres et indépendantes, il n'y a plus que de bas critiques d'art (espèce particulièrement gélatineuse) pour ne pas s'en apercevoir. Rien ne saurait exister en dehors des *caractères humains*, la réalité du monde extérieur elle-même doit se plier à cette exigence. Je veux bien admettre que, dans l'évolution des formes d'art, le déterminisme économique et social prédomine, tandis que l'humain se révèle plus puissamment dans son contenu et que les influences réciproques des formes sur les contenus puissent, à un moment donné de l'histoire, arriver à la résumer. Mais le résidu de cette œuvre, à n'importe quel moment de son évolution, restera toujours une quantité constante et c'est lui que nous avons en vue quand nous parlons de l'œuvre d'art. A l'amour de celle-ci préside le désir de retour à la vie pré-natale : le sentiment d'épanchement, de confort total et absolu, irrationnel, de l'absence de conscience et de responsabilité. Ce désir est de nature émotive, comme étant lié à l'angoisse du sentiment opposé, post-vital, représenté par la perte tragique, accidentelle, de la conscience. Autant il est doux de pouvoir se réfugier dans le premier, en sécurité, autant la crainte de ce dernier est liée à l'idée de violence. Dans l'appréciation de l'œuvre d'art, ce souvenir pré-natal qui est presque toujours le même chez tous les individus (lié aux satisfactions que donnent les substances à toucher, à lécher, à sucer, à croquer, à manger, à appliquer contre la peau ou la paupière, les substances chaudes, obscures, humides, etc.) est corrigé par les souvenirs d'enfance, qui, eux, imprègnent de leur grande variété les goûts et les dons d'observation, c'est-à-dire la spécialisation et la fixation des obsessions. Ceux qui se sont occupés d'objets d'art primitif, savent que les belles pièces présentent une usure dûe à l'attouchement prolongé qui ajoute à leur prix et à leur beauté, (usure répandue plus ou moins uniformément sur toute la surface, par conséquent non pas uniquement provoquée par des raisons d'ordre pratique de transport ou de déplacement), attouchement que le sauvage n'exerce pas pour évaluer des facteurs esthétiques dont il n'a que faire, mais pour répondre à une nécessité réelle, désir qui souvent prend la forme collective et policée d'un usage magique quelconque. (Egrener des chapelets, porter des cannes, etc... Dormir, chez les enfants, avec des objets à caractères totémiques, sucer certains jouets, etc., sont des phénomènes bien connus.) Ce qu'on appelle donc la *patine* des objets est une propriété infiniment précieuse, car elle est la confirmation que l'objet a déjà répondu aux désirs intra-utérins de toute une série d'individus et que, pour l'assouvissement de ceux-ci, il est réellement efficace. L'homme a besoin, pour apprécier une œuvre, de la vérification par des expériences tactiles précédentes exercées sur elle, expériences qui sont les formes concrètes des représentations intra-utérines. Il est évident que cette pratique amène un perfectionnement du processus de transfert par lequel les sensations tactiles et gustatives se font éprouver *visuellement*. (Le plus subtil

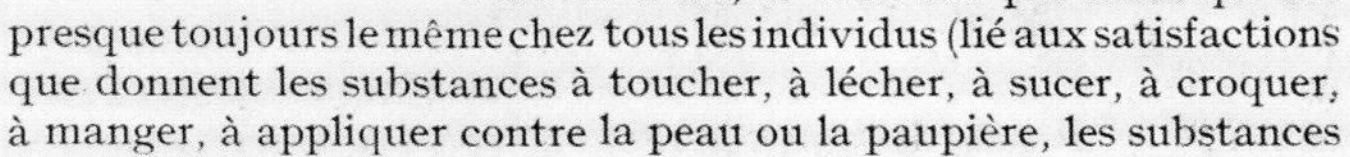

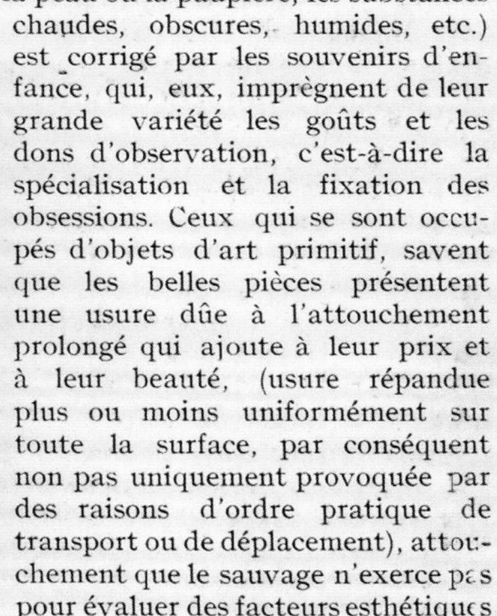

5. *Harper's Bazaar*, January 1937, p. 44. Photograph by Man Ray.

6. Man Ray, *Nusch Eluard, Fashion Photograph for Elsa Schiaparelli*, silver gelatin negative, c. 1930. Musée National d'Art Moderne – Centre de Création Industrielle, Paris, payment in kind 1994, inv. AM 1994-393 (4994).

folded tips equipped with a tie. In the very way that these, the two most distinctive accessories of male attire, the stretched garter conjuring up an image of virility and the tie whose symbolic role is known[26]—in the very way they surround the reproduction of the female sex which these women wear on their heads, one would have to be blind to miss not only the effect of fantasy filling the role of ingenious procuress, but a real justifying power with which the creators of these models endowed their works."[27] Man Ray photographed these small hats from above and diagonally to suggest their sexual forms (vulvas or breasts) and because Schiaparelli played along by posing in one of them,[28] it confirms her evident desire to participate in the article's provocative subject while helping to liberate women.

But beyond this spirit linking Man Ray and Schiaparelli, they both elevated their respective practices to the rank of art by using innovative techniques for the time. Man Ray, known for his highly personal works and photographic experiments, eventually transcended the art of portrait photography thanks to solarization. This laboratory accident, known since the nineteenth century as the "Sabatier effect," was perfected by Man Ray and his mastery of it made him hugely successful as of 1929. He also took a solarized portrait of Schiaparelli in 1934, giving her a mysterious aura. Man Ray also experimented by superimposing two negatives in the enlarger to create incongruous or significant juxtapositions. Man Ray thus put his inventiveness at the disposal of Schiaparelli (and fashion photography in general): overprinting allowed garments to be seen from different angles in the same photo, as in a photo published in *Harper's Bazaar* in March 1936,[29] another of a bride surrounded by lilies,[30] and that of an evening gown published in the January 1937 issue (ill. 5). He also used overhead angles to lengthen silhouettes and used pedestals in the manner of Brancusi.[31] Solarization idealized models as we see in his 1930's series featuring Nusch

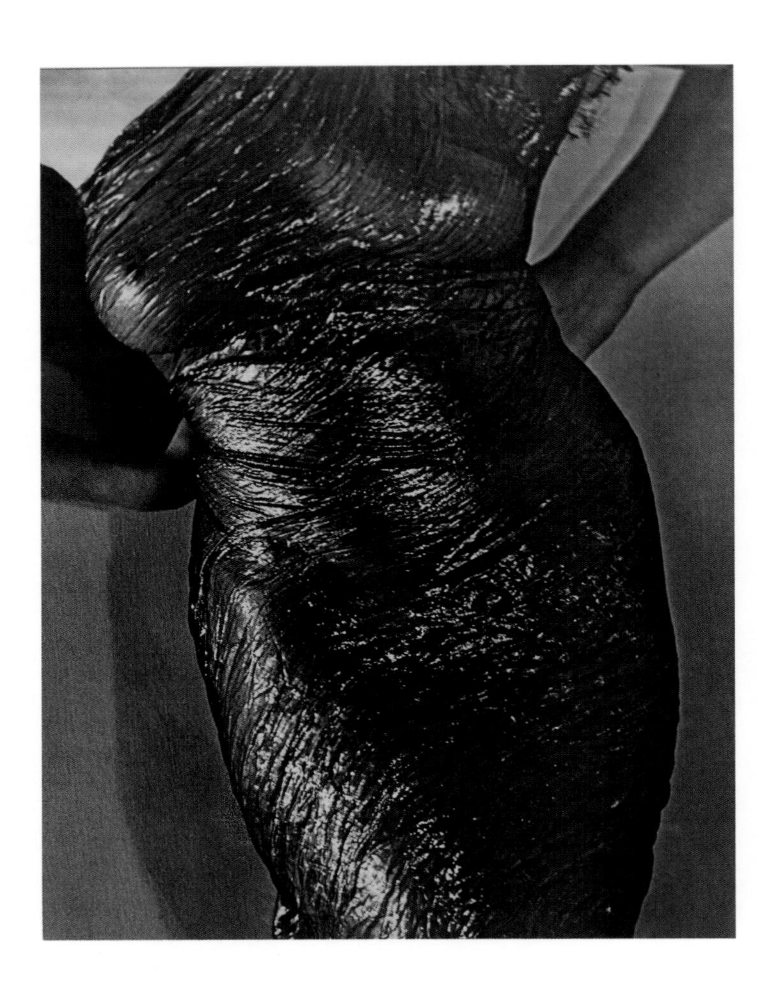

7. Man Ray, *Anatomies*, 1929, photograph. Bibliothèque Nationale de France, Paris, Département des Estampes et de la Photographie.

Eluard (ill. 6). Incongruous accessories gave the models a certain mystery, as with the wooden hand Man Ray used numerous times, notably for a portrait of Schiaparelli wearing a blond wig by the coiffeur Antoine in 1933,[32] a variation on the portrait with the bust (see p. 18). The same hairdresser appeared in Man Ray's illustrated report for *VU* magazine, "Le sculpteur de masques" (1933). All these effects contribute to going beyond the simple reproduction of a model into the realm of artistry while creating something dreamlike for the reader. As for Elsa Schiaparelli, she also made a name for herself as one of the greatest designers of her era thanks to her invention of new techniques—such as the aforementioned trompe l'oeil—and her use of new materials for her collections: a crinkle rayon crepe that resembled tree bark and Rhodophane, a material as transparent and fragile as glass. It should be noted that the choice of these unusual materials is similar to surrealist practices (such as *Object*, Meret Oppenheim's 1936 fur-covered cup, saucer, and spoon) and one of Man Ray's best-known photographs could have also been a source of inspiration: *Anatomy* (ill. 7), a nude female torso enveloped in a cellophane dress.

Nothing sheds light on or confirms these links, even though they are evident: no contract or official order. Just Man Ray's photographs. So, what can we deduce from all this? No doubt that during this period, artists formed a large, unified community where the ideas of one would stimulate others, and no one ever imagined creating a conflict with a peer about a few items that had been borrowed freely. *Fair weather* indeed!

1. Paul Poiret, known for his daring and considered the precursor of art deco style, opened his couture house in Paris in 1903.

2. Elsa Schiaparelli, *Shocking Life* (London: J. M. Dent & Sons, 1954), 5.

3. Ibid., 73.

4. Man Ray, *Self-Portrait* (Boston: Little, Brown and Company, 1963), 98–99.

5. Katherine Dreier, American artist and patron of the arts, particularly the Dada movement in New York. Her archives and collection are shared between the Yale University Gallery (a 1939 bequest), the Philadelphia Museum of Art (a 1952 bequest), and the Guggenheim Museum in New York (a 1953 bequest).

6. Berenice Abbott, an American artist, was a sculptor in New York at the time. After she arrived in Paris in 1923, she was his assistant before going off on her own to eventually become one of the most significant photographers of the twentieth century.

7. Do not misunderstand the term, it was not meant to be derogatory: Man Ray's mistress from 1936 to 1940 was the first black model in the history of fashion, Adrienne Fidelin, known as Ady.

8. The portrait in question is likely that of her in a blonde wig, face resting on a classical bust and reproduced in *Minotaure* 3–4 (December 1933): 4.

9. While Man Ray dedicated an entire chapter to Paul Poiret, he admitted that he had never taken his portrait. It has to be said that by 1925 Paul Poiret was extremely successful and was able to pay his photographers, while Schiaparelliwas still trying to find her way.

10. Schiaparelli, *Shocking Life*.

11. Ibid., 90.

12. This was the film *The Blood of a Poet*, made by Jean Cocteau in 1930.

13. Schiaparelli, *Shocking Life*, 98.

14. *La Femme de France*, September 27, 1931, 13.

15. Baron Georg von Hoyningen-Huene, known as George Hoyningen-Huene.

16. *Littérature*, October 1, 1922, 11.

17. Marcel Duchamp, *The Bride Stripped Bare by Her Bachelors, Even*, known as *The Large Glass*, 1915–23, Philadelphia Museum of Art, bequest of Katherine S. Dreier, oil, varnish, lead foil, lead wire, and dust on two glass panels, 277.5 × 177.8 × 8.6 cm.

18. [Isidore Ducasse, known as the] Comte de Lautréamont, *The Songs of Maldoror*, canto VI, in *Maldoror and Poems*, trans. Paul Knight (New York: Penguin, 1978), 216–17.

19. Bibliothèque Nationale de France collection.

20. André Breton, foreword to Man Ray, *La photographie n'est pas l'art* (Paris: GLM, 1937), unpaginated.

21. Dilys E. Blum, *Shocking! The Art and Fashion of Elsa Schiaparelli*, exh. cat. (Philadelphia: Philadelphia Museum of Art, 2003).

22. Man Ray, *Self-Portrait*, 297–98. There are two versions of this painting: the first from 1939 was sold at auction during the sale of Man Ray's studio in 1995 and is now in the Philadelphia Museum of Art; the second, painted by Man Ray in Hollywood in 1941 (he thought he had lost all the work he left behind in Paris during his chaotic departure in 1940), is now in a private collection.

23. *Minotaure* 3–4 (December 1933): 81–84. In one of the photos, Elsa poses in her hat (though not the "mad cap" for which she asked Man Ray to take other portraits).

24. This small knit hat, made in 1932, could take any shape.

25. Tristan Tzara, "Concerning a certain automatism of taste," in *The Surrealists Look at Art*, trans. Michael Palmer and Norma Cole (Venice, CA: Lapis Press, 1990), 205.

26. In his *Introduction to Psychoanalysis* (English translation, 1920), Sigmund Freud considered the tie a phallic symbol.

27. Tzara, "Concerning a certain automatism of taste," 205.

28. In the three images for the article presenting Elsa Schiaparelli's hats, one is on a recognizable head: her own (p. 83).

29. *Harper's Bazaar*, March 1936, 73.

30. *Harper's Bazaar*, April 1936, 115.

31. *Harper's Bazaar*, March 1936, 72–72a.

32. Musée Cantini, Marseille.

When Dalí Discovered Fashion

Jean-Louis Gaillemin

It was while writing "Les nouvelles couleurs du « sex appeal » spectral"[1] for a 1934 issue of *Minotaure* magazine that Dalí sketched out his vision of a woman of the future for the first time, a woman with an extra-flat, extra-thin, decomposed body. He announced the advent of the "spectral woman," who would be a "woman who could be taken apart . . . by disjointing and distorting her anatomy." He imagined bodies mounted "on claws" and "aerodynamic costumes." "All types of corsets will be updated for extra-fine uses and uncomfortable, anatomical, artificial pieces will be used to accentuate the atmospheric feeling of a breast, hip, or heel (extremely soft, well-molded though slightly sagging fake breasts that originate in the back, will be essential city outfits)." The disturbing *Female Beauty* by Alberto Martini, a spectral, flayed image of the Marchesa Casati, illustrated the article.

Dalí's delirious ideas about the spectral "woman of the future" can be seen in his painting *The Specter of Sex Appeal* (c. 1934), which he had just shown at the Galerie Bonjean. A monster kneels in front of Dalí, depicted as a frightened small boy wearing a sailor suit. The torn body with its distorted, mutilated limbs is only supported by crutches. The chimera's breasts and pelvis have been replaced by bags and a cushion held together by dirty fabric. Bones or excrement leak out of the skin, the right leg is truncated, the bare tibia is thrust in a piece of raw meat. During the same period, with the love of an umbrella (turgescent) and a sewing machine (castrating) as a theme, Dalí recounts the specter's avatars in his illustrations for *The Songs of Maldoror*.

This was when Dalí painted the first outfits of his "spectral" women. In his *Woman with a Head of Roses* (1935), the bouquet of roses emerges from a veil wrapped around the neck. Around her waist and on one of her arms, two caressing hands (in metal covered with fabric?) resemble a belt and a bracelet. On the hips of her companion, a belt made of chops encircles her waist. During his first stay in New York, Dalí showed the same hands caressing the waist and head of "an imaginary costume for a 'dream ball'" in *American Weekly*.[2] According to him, the hands represented "the desires of aviators."

The suit and coat with drawers

The suit with "drawer pockets" was the first collaboration between Schiaparelli and Dalí. On a 1936 drawing he gave her (ill. 2), Dalí noted: "Suit with semi-rigid, limp drawers, fabric imitating stripped oak, drawer handles in natural oak, for Schiaparelli, Her friend Salvador Dalí." This drawing was inspired by *The City of Drawers, or The Anthropomorphic Cabinet* painting he had just completed. Like the *Bizarreries* of the mannerist Bracelli, we see the torso of a nude woman lying on the ground made up of six drawers: two of the drawers are in the place of breasts and have nipple handles; the flat genitalia drawer only has one locked entrance. Whether the secret drawers of the unconscious or working-class jokes ("drop your drawers"), the comical rivals with the sadistic while feminine intimacy is laid bare. The drawer woman seems distressed, her face is hidden behind hair that simulates a vulva, a dirty cloth hangs out of her stomach drawer. A later drawing[3] shows her in the hysterical arched position of Charcot's mental patients at Hôpital de la Salpêtrière in Paris with boiled beans falling out of her stomach drawer.

1. Cover, *Minotaure*, no. 8, June 15, 1936. Illustration by Salvador Dalí.

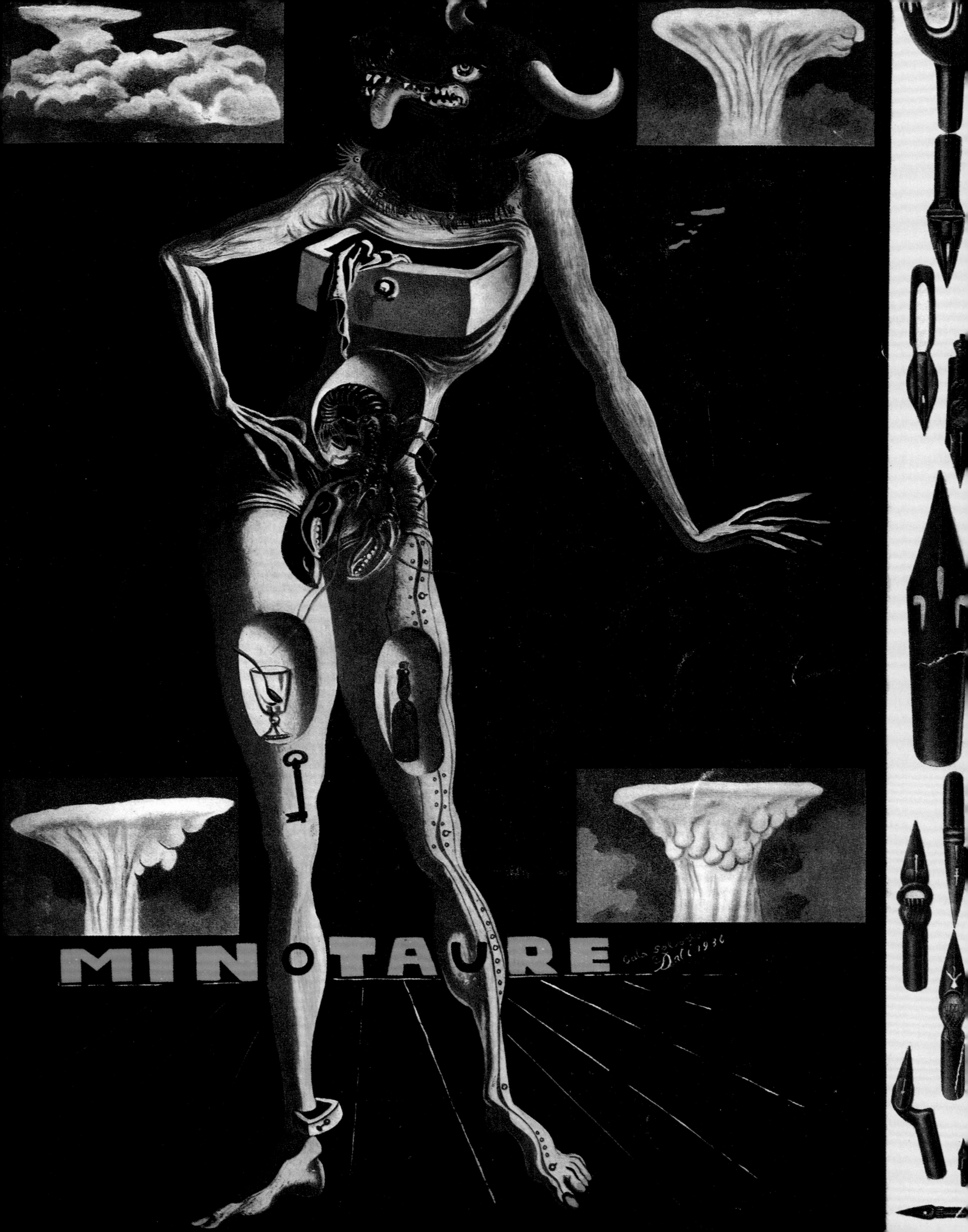
MINOTAURE
Gala
Dali 1936

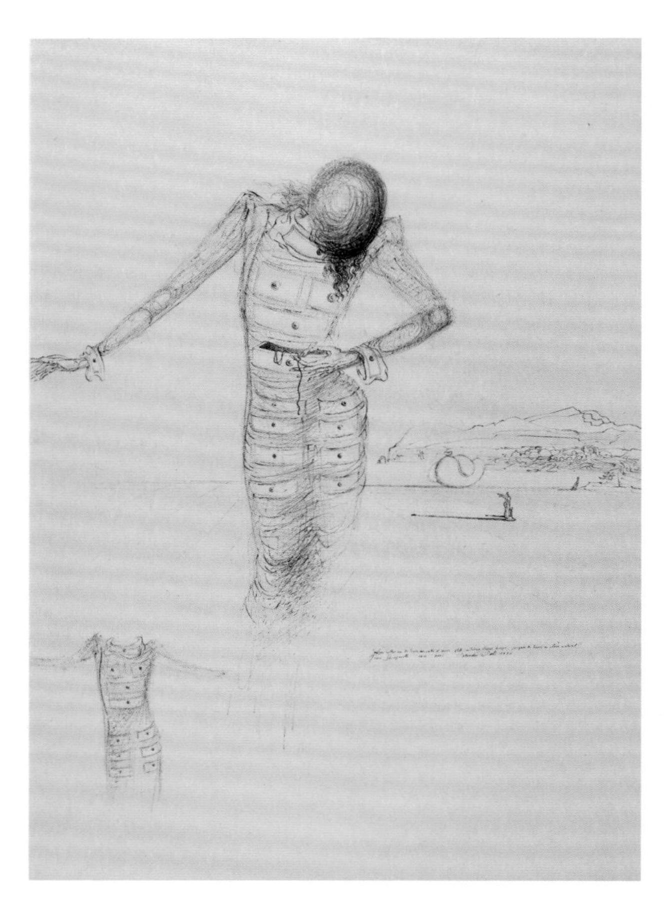

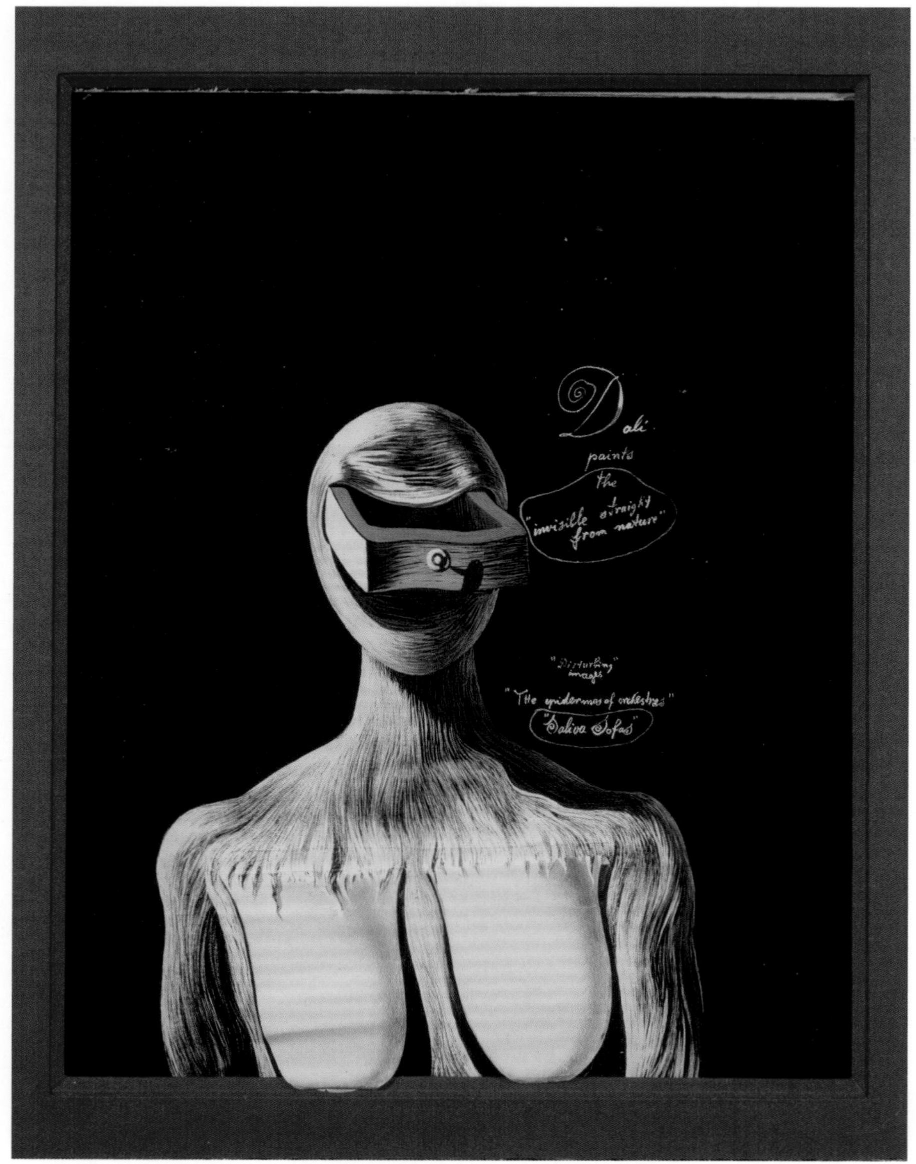
Dali
paints
the
"invisible straight
from nature"
"Disturbing"
images
"THe epidermis of orchestras"
"Saliva Sofas"

2. Salvador Dalí, *Woman with Drawers*, ink on paper, 1936. Maison Schiaparelli, Paris.

3. Salvador Dalí, *Woman-Drawer*, gouache on paper, 1936. Private collection, Paris.

4. *Vogue*, September 15, 1936, p. 70. Photograph by Cecil Beaton.

Dalí's gift to Schiaparelli of a suit sketch with drawers is more allusive. Although the breast drawers remain, the genitalia drawer has disappeared and, on the final garment made for the winter 1936–37 collection, the drawers of the torso skip the breasts while four others, placed symmetrically on the hips, do not allude to female genitalia. Despite not having its most obvious allusions, the coat was photographed by Cecil Beaton for *Vogue*[4] in a typical, Dalí-style, deserted beach setting (ill. 4). One of the models hold the latest issue of *Minotaure*. On the magazine's cover (by Dalí), we see a minotaur with drawers or rather "a female minotaur" with a hybrid, part-wolf, part-bull head with carnivorous teeth waiting to bite (ill. 1). A diabolical lobster surges out of a troubling cavity under the breast whose pincers are ready to open and protect the intimate labyrinth inside. Theseus who was about to have a manly fight, had to be careful. The drawer fashion was so successful that Dalí and Bettina Bergery—who collaborated with Schiaparelli on her window displays—placed a polar bear dyed shocking pink with a drawer in its stomach in the Schiaparelli boutique window on the Place Vendôme. Dalí's *Venus de Milo with Drawers*, which he did the same year, showed the success of these body-inspired objects with the public, the handles were replaced by delicious white mink pompoms that subtly caressed the plaster statue.

5. George Platt Lynes, *Salvador Dalí*, gelatin silver print with applied pigment, 1939. Metropolitan Museum of Art, New York, David Hunter McAlpin Fund, 1941, inv. 41.65.28.

6. Elsa Schiaparelli, lobster dress, February 1937 collection. Philadelphia Museum of Art, Philadelphia, gift of Elsa Schiaparelli, 1969, inv. 1969-232-52.

The lobster dress

Appearing on the head of a strange spy in the painting *Gala and the Angelus of Millet* in 1933, the lobster also decorated Gala's head (*Portrait of Gala with a Lobster*, 1933) and, in 1934, Dalí devised for *American Weekly*[5] his first lobster telephone where a frightened man tries to put his hand on the putrid lobster that has replaced the earpiece. The following year, Dalí recreated his *Woman with a Head of Roses* painting in the Bonwit Teller store window in New York. It features his first lobster telephone perched on an anthropomorphic cabinet. From organized cracks in the walls emerged the arms of the woman's admirers who held either gifts or threatening objects.

Although, in the end, the drawers' erotic allusions went unnoticed, the same was not the case for Schiaparelli's lobster dress in the summer of 1937 (ill. 6). Here the crustacean emerging from the stomach of the castrating "female minotaur" surges from the model's crotch onto immaculate white silk. Certainly, this new lobster was less terrifying than the female minotaur but the lobster's placement is clear as seen in a photograph of Wallis Simpson by Cecil Beaton for *Vogue*[6] shortly before her marriage. Was the future Duchess of Windsor so naive as to not notice the hidden erotic message behind the humorous nature of the dress? Or did she instead use the occasion to assert her reputation as an independent, manipulative woman?

The torn dress

Elsa Schiaparelli, who had adored *Woman with a Head of Roses*, owned two paintings depicting it: *Dreams Puts Her Hand on a Man's Shoulder* (1936) and *Necrophilic Spring* (1936), both gifts from Dalí. We can wonder if this new character in Dalí's mythology resulted from his intimate conversations with the designer. In her autobiography, she recounts that as a little girl, crushed by her sister's stunning beauty, she "thought up ways of beautifying herself. To have a face covered with flowers like a heavenly garden would indeed be a wonderful thing! And if she could make flowers sprout all over her face. . . . With some difficulties she obtained seeds from the gardener, and these she planted in her throat, ears, mouth. . . . Alas, in this matter-of-fact world, the result was merely to make Schiap suffocate."[7] It was in these two paintings that slashed, torn fabric appeared for the first time. In *Dreams Puts Her Hand on a Man's Shoulder*, the dream wears clothing in rags. In another painting, *Three Young Surrealist Women Holding in Their Arms the Skins of an Orchestra* (ill. 8), the irregularly torn fabric reveals skin and stands out against the immaculate dress. On Schiaparelli's definitive summer 1938 dress,[8] all these bodily allusions are erased (ill. 7). The tears, now bigger, do not reveal skin but rather a pink lining. Only the printed fabric of the dress inside, visible in the tears, is ambiguous: Is it animal fur or torn skin? The woman with a head of roses appeared in Trafalgar Square in 1936 and was incarnated by Sheila Legge during the London surrealist exhibition.

7. Design drawing, evening dress, summer 1938 collection. Musée des Arts Décoratifs, Paris, gift of Elsa Schiaparelli, Ufac, 1973, inv. UF d 73-21-3747.

8. Salvador Dalí, *Three Young Surrealist Women Holding in Their Arms the Skins of an Orchestra* (detail), painting, 1936. The Dalí Museum, St. Petersburg, Florida, inv. P 418.

9. Elsa Schiaparelli, evening dress known as the "skeleton dress," summer 1938 (2017 reproduction). Maison Schiaparelli, Paris.

10. Design drawing, evening dress known as the "skeleton dress," summer 1938 collection. Musée des Arts Décoratifs, Paris, gift of Elsa Schiaparelli, Ufac, 1973, inv. UF d 73-21-1874.

The skeleton dress

What better "surrealist" idea than to reverse the relationship of the skeleton to the body and imagine a human being sheltered by a carapace where it benefits from the voluptuousness Dalí gave the fantastic lobster? A drawing Dalí gave Schiaparelli in 1938 was accompanied by a letter: "Dear Elsa, I truly love the idea of 'outside bones' so here are two handbag designs to go with the suit. See you tomorrow evening, regards from your Dalí." (ill. 10) Elsewhere in the drawing, an enigmatic piece of jewelry "must be laced at the navel to accentuate the 'hornemental' character of the interlacing." But when considering the details of these "skeleton dresses," it is not easy to find the bony details. It is more the "limp" version of Dalí's skeleton like the one depicted in 1929 in *Memory of the Woman-Child* and in the *Spectre of Sex Appeal* avatar that was seen in the *Javanais Mannequin* (c. 1934).

Although the lower, anamorphosed limbs show their bones, including a bare one, the torso is just a limp, round rib cage. Here the limpness and curves characterize the bones of the drawing and help us understand the organic shapes of the two bags. The fabulous sewing technique of trapunto stitching with two layers of fabric and padding helped create the snake-like volumes that caress more than imprison the model (ill. 9).

The shoe hat

11. *L'Officiel*, October 1937, p. 38. Photograph by Georges Saad.

Your little tootsies, playing footsie—many expressions and metaphors make women's shoes a favorite with fetishists. From the strange shoes of Rembrandt's *Danaë*, which seem to wait, like their comforting mistress, to be rained down upon by Jupiterian gold, to David Lynch's Louboutin-shod nude models, images abound that focus not only on the openness of the shoe, but also the strength and phallic authority conferred by the high heel. Dalí himself was not to be outdone. In his 1931 article on objects with a symbolic function,[9] he describes his *Scatological Object with a Symbolic Function (Gala's Shoe)* as "a woman's shoe inside of which I placed a warm glass of milk in the center of a paste in a ductile shape that was the color of excrement." This is located inside an infernal machine whose setting in motion entails a meticulous ritual: "The mechanism consists of dipping a sugar cube painted with the image of a shoe to observe the sugar's disintegration and, eventually, the shoe's image disappearing in the milk. Various accessories (pubic hair glued to a piece of sugar, a small erotic photo) complete the object."

The woman's shoe appeared in painting during this period, furtive, hidden in paintings as if it made us afraid.[10] We can guess at its presence under a shrouds draped over the young, ashamed man Dalí incarnated in the summer of 1933 in Man Ray's photograph: wearing a shoe on his head or neck as he poses "upside down," the shoes are objects of desire and shame. Two depicted here, with their heels placed on the toes of a phantom Dalí, even provoke a shameful practice that the shroud can barely hide.

Dalí's sketched proposals for the shoe hat[11] play with curves and arches without realistic details, a pure, formal allusion ultimately found in Schiaparelli's final object made all in black (ill. 11). Only the shocking pink heel adds a provocative accent. Though the hat was extremely successful as an image, few clients were daring enough to wear it. We see a leopard skin version of the shoe hat worn by Katherine Helmond in Terry Gilliam's movie *Brazil* (1985), another example of an upside-down world.

Schiaparelli's mastery of couture techniques always meant that she could temper Dalí's delirious ideas in the final object, even if some, as the designer recalls, were used, above all, to generate publicity: "There were another hat resembling a lamb cutlet with a white frill on the bone, and this, more than anything else, contributed to Schiap's fame for eccentricity. She wore it defiantly and certain newspaper columnists have never forgotten it."[12]

1. *Minotaure* 5 (May 12, 1934): 20–22.

2. "The American City Night-and-Day by Dalí," *American Weekly*, March 31, 1935.

3. *The Hysterical Arch*, 1937, The Dalí Museum, St. Petersburg, Florida.

4. *Vogue*, September 15, 1936, 70.

5. "New York as Seen by the 'Super-Realist' Artist, M. Dalí," *American Weekly*, February 24, 1935.

6. *Vogue*, June 1, 1937, p. 52-57.

7. Elsa Schiaparelli, *Shocking Life* (London: J.M. Dent & Sons, 1954), 6–7.

8. Philadelphia Museum of Art, Philadelphia, inv. 1969-232-45 a,b.

9. Salvador Dalí, "Objets à fonctionnement symbolique," *Le Surréalisme au service de la révolution* 3 (December 1931).

10. We think notably of *Fish Man* (1930), Meadows Museum, Southern Methodist University, Dallas, Texas; *The Sense of Speed* (1931), Fundació Gala-Salvador Dalí, Figueres; and *Premature Ossification of a Railroad Station* (1931), private collection.

11. Winter 1937–38, The Metropolitan Museum of Art, New York, inv. 1974.139.

12. Schiaparelli, *Shocking Life*, 97–98.

Three Asides

Patrick Mauriès

I

In 1937 Jean Cocteau pinned a phrase to the creative approach of the Place Vendôme couturiere—"Madame Schiaparelli has taken literally the expression: the theatre of the mode [*sic*]." (He was to use the phrase again eight years, and one war, later in another context, as we shall see.) His article "From Worth to Alix" was published in the March issue of *Harper's Bazaar*, and sketched a panorama of Parisian fashion from the start of the century, with his own childhood memories, to the latest folly of the day, the fashion of Alix, the future Madame Grès. It offered a quietly Hegelian sequence of innovations and excess, from Worth to Poiret, from Poiret to Chanel, and from Chanel to Schiaparelli, with Alix bringing the spectacle to a close.

Time having done its work, we tend to forget, today, that the notorious "Chanel-Courrèges match," the subject of a famous essay by Roland Barthes in 1967, was preceded, thirty years earlier, by the no less combative one between Chanel and Schiaparelli. Cocteau was a first-hand witness to it, as he was close to both adversaries, as indeed he was to the entire Parisian circle. Chanel, who, according to him, was the priestess of "glorious invisibility," preaching "*violent* simplicity" embodied by the "beige uniform of knitted wool" that liberated women as it erased their figures, did away definitively with the intricacy of bayadere silk in the early 1920s. Fifteen years later, however, she, in turn, found herself confronted with a "sharp and tumultuous" reaction to a weariness of neutral tones and uniform, and to avoid being left behind, was "obliged to turn her imagination toward folies" to which she abandoned herself so she could control them all the better.

Schiaparelli presented the new face of a fashion whose impermanence was its very reason for existing. "The masquerade began," Cocteau resumed laconically, before throwing himself into an inspired tirade: "Schiaparelli is above all the dressmaker of eccentricity. Has she not the air of a young demon who tempts women, who leads the mad carnival in a burst of laughter? Her establishment in the Place Vendôme is a devil's laboratory. Women who go there fall into a trap, and come out masked, disguised, deformed, or reformed, according to Schiaparelli's whim. The richest laces alternate with the most austere cassocks and the braid of toreadors."

We'll come back to the singular, or singularly feminine, nature of the Place Vendôme coven as sketched by Cocteau. But we might also ask ourselves about Chanel's reaction to this portrait and to the importance given to the woman she referred to as "the Italian," who she did not exactly view with kindness (to the extent of steering her toward the flames of a candelabrum when she appeared in costume as a "surrealist oak tree" at the Bal de la Forêt hosted by André Durst in 1939).

Schiaparelli only appeared on the fashion scene a decade or so before the publication of Cocteau's essay. Cocteau himself had been linked to Chanel in a lengthy trade-off dating back to the end of World War I and their shared visits to the Ballet Russes. She had offered him her support on many occasions, without actually approving of the excesses of the opium-addicted poet. She had paid for the funeral costs of Cocteau's unhappy lover Raymond Radiguet in 1923, and for the poet's drug treatment at the end of 1928, lending him an apartment in Rue Cambon before welcoming him at La Pausa, her villa above Roquebrune, in 1929, and settling his debts on numerous occasions. She also designed the costumes for several of his plays and librettos: *Antigone* in 1922, *Le Train bleu* in 1924, *Orpheus*

1. Elsa Schiaparelli in collaboration with Jean Cocteau, evening coat, fall 1937 collection. Philadelphia Museum of Art, Philadelphia, gift of Elsa Schiaparelli, 1969, inv. 1969-232.

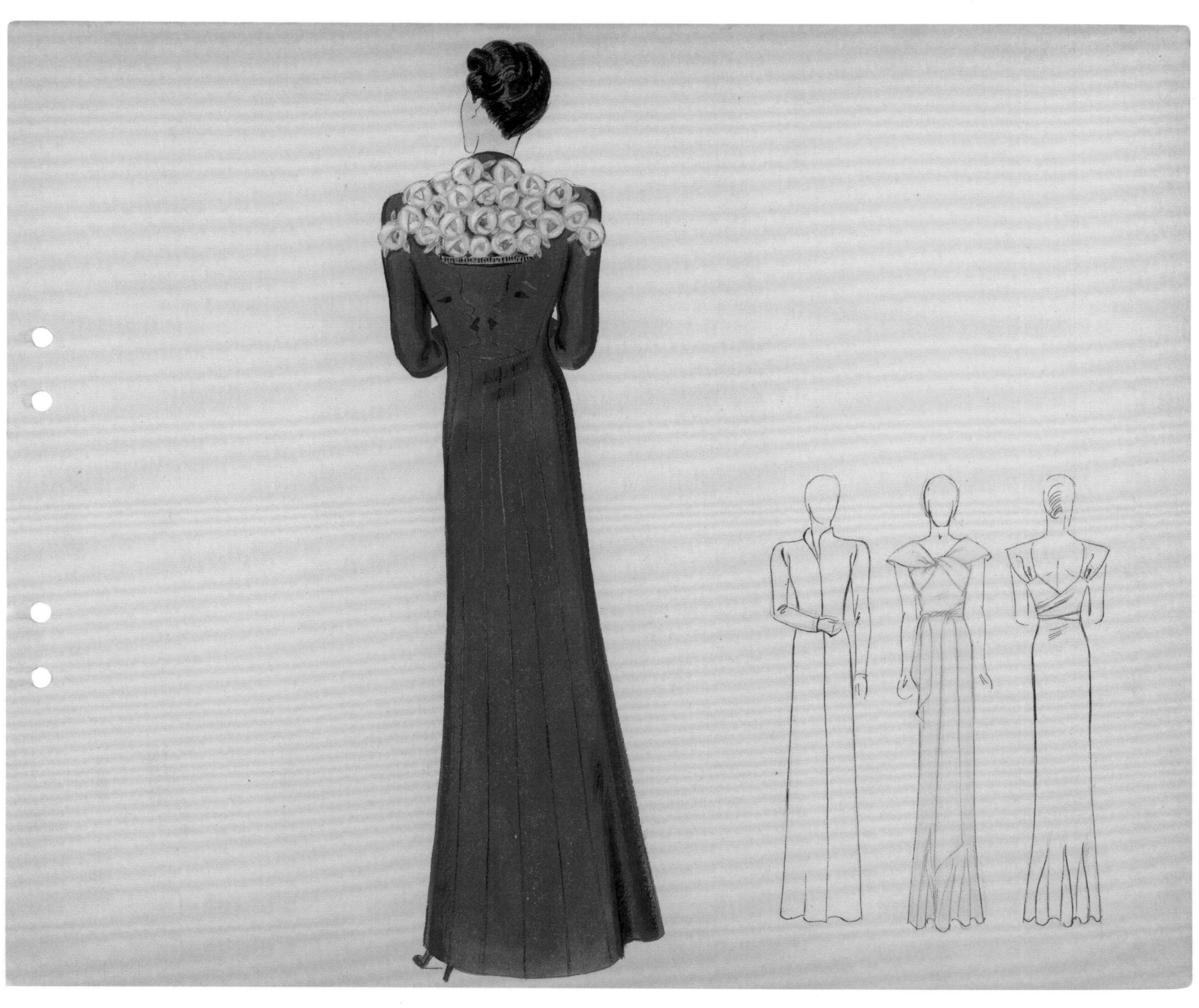

2. Jean Cocteau, drawing, c. 1936. West Dean College of Arts and Conservation, Chichester, inv. EJA/1/22/8a.

3. Design drawing, evening coat, fall 1937 collection. Musée des Arts Décoratifs, Paris, gift of Elsa Schiaparelli, Ufac, 1973, inv. UF d 73-21-1714.

in 1926, *The Infernal Machine* in 1934, and *The Knights of the Round Table* in 1937.

As the newcomer, Schiaparelli's presence in this friendship may have been like a bull in a china shop. That did not prevent her, as she said in her memoirs, from seeing "him often . . . this man, who seems not a man but a pure spirit, with a gift for conversation that cracks every other person present into silence." As for Cocteau, in tune as he was with the spirit of the times, he immediately recognized in her the embodiment of a new sensibility, already seen in the famous trompe l'oeil sweater that accidentally launched her career in 1928, and which displayed her taste for the incongruous and for playful connivance. This was a major source of discord with Chanel who, as a former milliner, viewed her profession as a craft, as know-how, while Schiaparelli favored the notion of a "shock" effect, an event, a movement, an idea, from which the execution would follow. Far from wishing to be invisible and functional, her creations were essentially visual and provocative, engaging the viewer's eye in a game that existed thanks to the garment and the person wearing it, the "actress" in all senses of the word. Which is why Schiaparelli was interested in artists from the start of her career—in addition to Cocteau, she befriended Salvador Dalí, Leonor Fini, Christian Bérard, Raoul Dufy, Kees van Dongen, Alberto Giacometti, Marcel Vertès, Étienne Drian, and Eric, not forgetting Jean Schlumberger.

As she wrote in *Shocking Life*, "Working with artists like Bebe [*sic*] Bérard, Jean Cocteau, Salvador Dalí, Vertès, Van Dongen; and with photographers like Hoyningen-Hueni [*sic*], Horst, Cecil Beaton, and Man Ray gave one a sense of exhilaration. One felt supported and understood beyond the crude and boring reality of merely making a dress to sell." In Schiaparelli's eyes, fashion was "justified" by these varied contributions, be it in the design of models (Cocteau) or in the field of printed fabrics, so well-exploited before her by Poiret (Dalí, Bérard, Dufy, Vertès, van Dongen), or in what today we call the couture house's visual identity, from promotional imagery (Bérard, van Dongen, Vertès) to the design of accessories (Leonor Fini).

Like her, Cocteau knew that the particularity of looking was to allow oneself to be deceived. All his work was traversed by the theme of the double, of reflection, of metamorphosis, and of mirrors "that would do well to reflect a little more before sending back images." (It is interesting to note that Schiaparelli made this doubling the stylistic device of her memoirs, which are as if written alternately by herself and an alter ego named Schiap, in an unabashedly schizophrenic manner.)

It is thus not surprising that the two models that Cocteau designed for Schiaparelli, the same year as his article about her was published, have to do with an optical illusion or magic. In the first, the profile of a woman is traced on a linen evening jacket, her abundant hair of pure gold thread contrasting with the austere fabric as it tumbles down the right arm of the jacket in an asymmetrical fashion, while two hands encircle her waist (ills. 4 and 5). (The hand, an instrument for conjuring and legerdemain, featured regularly in Schiaparelli's work, inspiring brooches, buttons, and a pair of gloves with embroidery spiritually representing the hands covered.)

Cocteau's second model, a silk jersey coat expertly embroidered by Albert Lesage, uses an image that can be read in two ways: either as two faces turned toward each other or as a vase with old-fashioned pink taffeta flowers opening out into a bouquet on the shoulders (ills. 2 and 3). Cocteau designed them for the fall 1937 collection, as a prelude to the extraordinary sequence he created the following year, starting with Circus in February, Pagan in April, Zodiac in August, and Commedia dell'arte in October, marking the height of the couturiere's career.

Schiaparelli herself was perfectly aware of embodying the "new spirit" that Cocteau evoked in such a lyrical fashion, as well as that which opposed it to the spirit of the previous decade, to its rigorism. Referring to the 1920s, and taking a shot at Chanel in passing, she wrote: "It was the time when abstract Dadaism and Futurism were the talk of the world, the time when chairs looked like tables, and tables like footstools, when it was not done to ask what a painting represented or what a poem meant, when trifles of fantasy were taboo and only the initiated knew about the Paris Flea Market, when women had no waists, wore paste jewellery, and compressed their bust to look like boys." Schiaparelli and Cocteau were not alone in weighing up the consequences of this analysis. Proof of this is found in statements by such diverse characters as the American musician Virgil Thomson and the journalist Madge Garland, an unjustly forgotten figure of fashion history, and an exacting but ephemeral editor of British *Vogue*. In an overview of the 1930s, published in 1968, she wrote: "Early in the thirties a reaction took place against the visual austerity of the twenties when simplification reached its zenith, when functionalism was the watchword, and when the house was conceived as a 'machine to live in.'" The "double reading" of Cocteau's designs perfectly expressed the desire to escape this constraint and reconnect with even the "slightest of whims" that the 1938 collections developed with dazzling virtuosity.

As expressions of a vision of existence as theater, the couturiere's creations were naturally meant for the stage, and she became the interpreter of Cocteau's poetic universe with her designs for Jany Holt's costumes in *Les Monstres sacrés*, which premiered at the Théâtre Michel on February 17, 1940. The actress was photographed by Man Ray in the April issue of *Harper's Bazaar*, wearing a long white crepe gown borrowed from the Pagan collection—a modern Norma with her belt and tiara of shadowy foliage. Like the actress's other outfits—black satin pajama pants with an embroidered jacket and a dress with large roses on a black background—these creations contrasted superbly with the different tones of red used for the sets. These costumes, like all those made for the theater, were ephemeral, leaving less of a trace than those used for the renowned Robert Bresson film *The Ladies of the Bois de Boulogne* made in 1945, for which Cocteau wrote the dialogues. Here, in sharp contrast to the costumes of *Les Monstres sacrés*, with their pillbox hats, hoods, veils, and muffs, it is the deep, velvety black of the harshly baroque outfits for Élina Labourdette, Lucienne Bogaert, and the intriguing Maria Casarès that enhance the sense of mystery, deepened by the play of light. It is difficult not to see in the brooding, stylized figure played by Casarès a foreshadowing of the "Princess" that she was to embody five years later in Cocteau's *Orpheus*.

4. Design drawing, evening ensemble, fall 1937 collection. Musée des Arts Décoratifs, Paris, gift of Elsa Schiaparelli, Ufac, 1973, inv. UF d 73-21-1711.

5. Elsa Schiaparelli in collaboration with Jean Cocteau, evening jacket, fall 1937 collection. Philadelphia Museum of Art, Philadelphia, inv. 1969-232-22.

II

The vibrant red that set the scenery of *Les Monstres sacrés* ablaze was one of Christian Bérard's favorite colors (ill. 7); the same color is found in brilliant flat tints in his famous portrait of Tamara Toumanova, painted in 1931. Bérard was a close friend of Cocteau and had worked with him since the 1920s. Before working with Schiaparelli on this production, he had found favor with her, possibly more so than any other artist. She involved him in her work very early on, commissioning printed and embroidered fabrics from him. This was particularly the case, as Palmer White wrote in his 1986 monograph, "for the magnificent Roi Soleil cape first modelled by Daisy Fellowes" and that later formed part of the Zodiac collection.

Bérard also became the visual chronicler of her creations. After leaving *Harper's Bazaar* for *Vogue* in 1935 (while continuing to send drawings to the former under the pseudonym of Sam, according to Carmel Snow, the magazine's editor), he regularly depicted Schiaparelli's models for the catwalk reports, notably dedicating a magnificent page to the Circus collection in 1938, the inspiration for which he was certainly no stranger to. The painter's flamboyant beard ("peopled with various creatures," according to Carmel Snow) even provided Schiaparelli with the inspiration for an unusual "bearded hat," as we read in *Vogue* in May 1940—a discreet sign of their "strange collaboration," its skullcap extended in an artful bil-

6. *Harper's Bazaar*, April 1935, p. 62. Photograph by George Hoyningen-Huene.
Model wearing a Schiaparelli evening ensemble posing in front of the folding screen made by Christian Bérard for Elsa Schiaparelli.

7. Design drawing, cape and evening dress, fall 1936 collection. Musée des Arts Décoratifs, Paris, gift of Elsa Schiaparelli, Ufac, 1973, inv. UF d 73-21-148.
The fabric for this dress was designed by Christian Bérard.

low of tulle tied below the chin, giving new meaning to the French expression *collier de barbe* ("chinstrap" or, literally, "beard necklace").

Schiaparelli judged Bérard less severely than did Edna Woolman Chase, the categorical director of American *Vogue*, for she appreciated him as a painter as much as an illustrator and theater designer. One of her most precious possessions was the screen in front of which she often posed for photographs, which, as she recounts in her memoirs, was the result of a quid pro quo (ill. 6). "He was dining one evening at my house in the Rue Barbet de Jouy. I was still in the process of decorating it, and the big hall was so draughty that I asked him if he would paint me a small screen to put in front of the door. 'Certainly', he answered, 'but can you pay me in advance? I am broke.' 'Of course.'" There followed a month, then two, of waiting and disappointment, of awkwardness and then tension, ending in a scene between the two protagonists where it transpired that there had been a simple imbroglio. The valet of the elderly marquise who owned the house in which Schiaparelli lived and who herself dabbled in painting, had intercepted the screen upon delivery, wishing to save the marquise from a nasty shock ("'Madame la Marquise also paints, you see, and this thing . . .' He threw up his hands in horror!!"). Schiaparelli had never seen the screen, and Bérard had taken her lack of reaction as a rejection.

"The screen," she continued, "was a beauty, and one of the best things that Bebe [*sic*] ever did. He had put immense feeling and skill in it. Done in the manner of an Italian fresco, there were three panels of the Virgin and her pages." Given that the latter, nowadays, are seen as androgynous angels rather than pages, in keeping with a recurrent motif chez Bérard (they also feature, curiously, in the British and American editions of *Shocking Life*), we are able to appreciate, like Schiaparelli, what a remarkable work this was, serving as yet further proof of the link between the designer and the new spirit of the times.

This new aesthetic, which had been branded as "neo-romantic," more or less appropriately, by the art critic Waldemar George in 1926, had found in Bérard and some of his fellow students, including the painters Pavel Tchelitchew, Eugène Berman, and Leonid Berman, all of Russian origin, its most talented representatives. Schiaparelli's work, with its predilection for trompe l'oeil, allusions, references, and ironic reinterpretations, can be seen as the extension of this sensibility within the field of fashion as much as of surrealism to which she is traditionally linked.

Schiaparelli's affection for Bérard is felt in the portrait she gives of him in *Shocking Life* (for which he designed the tailpieces), that merits being quoted at length: "When Bérard walked so lightly into a crowded room, yes, so lightly in spite of his corpulence, a beatific smile almost lost in his vast beard, swinging forward with the impalpable grace of an elephant, his little white dog Jacinthe under his arm, the whole atmosphere became charged. His arrival would immediately become known in the mannequin cabin. The show could start.

"If he liked the show he made remarks in a loud voice. His enthusiasm was immense and everybody was caught up by it. I am quite sure that many ideas became popular and sold well because Bebe kept on repeating: 'C'est divin! C'est divin!'

"As a man he was too gifted. He was apt to neglect his career as a painter to do things that merely amused him. The theatre occupied much of his time, and some of his scenery, like that for *L'École des femmes* and *La Symphonie fantastique*, was extremely beautiful. He loved theatre and in a theatre he died."

How appropriate that the last collaboration between Bérard and Schiaparelli, several months before the former's death, should have been devising some final stage sets—those intimate, miniature ones Bérard created for the "theatre of the mode [*sic*]" show in 1945. It was intended to promote French fashion after the war and served as the setting for dolls dressed by the leading couturieres of the day, in tableaux with themes described by Cocteau, who went on to group them together in the phrase he had so aptly devised a few years earlier in reference to Schiaparelli.

III

Leonor Fini also made herself heard in matters of theater (remember Paul Eluard's famed remark: "When it's Fini ['finished' in French], it starts!"). It's surprising, therefore, how little trace there appears to be of her inevitable encounters with Bérard—be it in the world of fashion or high society—to whom she was so close in terms of subject matter and imagination. Fini came to Paris in 1931 and was introduced to Schiaparelli by Christian Dior who, at that time, together with his associate Pierre Colle, owned a gallery representing Dalí, de Chirico, and the neo-romantics. The understanding between the young artist, recently arrived from Trieste, and the couturiere, much in vogue at that time, was apparently immediate. These two Italian women, each as powerful and explosive as the other, seemed to be made to get on. In 1936 Fini made an admirable portrait of Gogo, Schiaparelli's daughter, in the elegant, icy, neo-mannerist vein that was hers at that stage, before making another, even more remarkable one, three years later, of Jean Schlumberger, the couturiere's appointed jewelry designer, displaying his creations like a late Renaissance artist.

The affinity between the two artists could be seen in the fashion press in 1939, notably in the September issue of *Harper's Bazaar*. In a photograph by Hoyningen-Huene, one of Schiaparelli's models—a long black crepe gown belted with a daring pouf-like muff trimmed with an artistically-tied pink bow—is displayed in front of a strange piece of fretwork furniture (ill. 8). Leonor Fini had designed this "angel wardrobe" for the inaugural exhibition of a gallery next to the Schiaparelli showrooms in

8. *Harper's Bazaar*, September 1939, p. 67. Photograph by George Hoyningen-Huene.

Place Vendôme owned by René Drouin, future champion of Jean Dubuffet and Simon Hantaï, and his associate, a young man from Trieste named Leo Castelli, whose story needs no telling.

This wardrobe, modern in style, was composed of two winged caryatids whose hair billowed upward, joining at the top. It was part of a group of fantasy furniture that included Meret Oppenheim's henceforth famous bird-footed table and Eugène Berman's illusionist wardrobe, now in the Victoria and Albert Museum. Fini was the advisor, if not the instigator, behind this exhibition in which she also displayed two painted panels representing "painting" and "architecture," inspired by the grotesque costumes of the engraver Nicolas II de Larmessin, and a spiritual corset chair in metal, echoes of which were found elsewhere.

The similarity between the two designers is further corroborated in three superb illustrations published in *Harper's Bazaar* in 1939 and 1940. The first one shows a long red velvet dress with a large two-tone ribbon from the winter 1939 collection; the second, an evening dress in midnight blue with a "sleeping blue" bolero embellished with jet, and the third, a dinner dress yet again in "sleeping blue" with a high waist fitted snugly around a tyrian purple blouse, were from the summer 1940 collection. These images, with the models arranged in a no man's land typical of Fini, peopled with sphynxes and hybrid creatures against a dappled sky, contrast with the norms of fashion illustration, forming proper pictorial compositions that reinforce the complicity, if not the common aesthetic between the two women.

Two years' earlier, Fini had created an original hat box for Schiaparelli's somewhat eccentric models at the behest of Alexey Brodovitch, the admirable artistic director of *Harper's Bazaar*, who had also asked Cassandre, Giorgio

9. Ad for Shocking perfume. Photograph by Arik Népo.

10. The American actress and singer Mae West.

de Chirico, and Miguel Covarrubias to do the same. But the most visible trace of Fini's collaboration with Schiaparelli is undoubtedly the bottle for the couturiere's perfume Shocking, behind which looms the swaying, luxuriant shadow of Mae West.

Referring to West's sudden appearance in her atelier, Schiaparelli's memoirs take a surgical turn that Maldoror would not have been averse to: "Mae West came to Paris. She was stretched out on the operating-table of my work-room, and measured and probed with care and curiosity. She had sent me all the most intimate details of her famous figure, and for greater accuracy a plaster statue of herself quite naked in the pose of the Venus de Milo." Nowadays, with the likes of the Kardashians, it's difficult to imagine the actress's capacity for provocation and scandal in the first half of the twentieth century, that stemmed less from her art of bawdy insinuation than her manner of assuming an aloof form of femininity to the point of being threatening (it was no accident that she inspired Salvador Dalí as well as John Waters). West represented, in an almost military fashion, the exact opposite of the female archetype of the previous decade with its absence of hips and bust flattened with the help of elastic bandages. She managed to impose an "hourglass figure" (ill. 10), one of the unexpected consequences of which was, as Schiaparelli confirmed, the vogue for "falsies," those false breasts, the "most modern" of which could be blown up with a straw "as if . . . sipping crème de menthe."

Schiaparelli continued: "From this silhouette also arose the bottle of perfume shaped like a woman, that famous Schiaparelli bottle that practically became the signature of the house. Eleanore Fini [*sic*] modelled it for me and the scent took more than a year to be ready." In the shape of a woman's bust or a Stockman mannequin adorned with a tape measure and a bunch of flowers presented beneath a plastic cloche evoking Victorian wedding bouquets (ill. 9), Fini's bottle added a motif to the repertory of body parts that single out the couturiere's universe—from lip-buttons to hand-belts and gloves that we have already mentioned. The female figures in Fini's pictures featured the same hourglass figures at that time, and she and Schiaparelli shared a taste for the redrawn, exaggerated, "deformed or remodeled" bodies that Cocteau referred to, as well as costumes and fancy dress, or rather, a detachment, a doubling of the body that gives itself a second skin, that becomes the metaphor. We recognize the "mad carnival [led] in a burst of laughter" in the "devil's laboratory" of the Place Vendôme: sabbath, circus, or merry-go-round of masks, striges, and griffins where triumphant femininity is exalted, jubilant, and liberated.

Note on the text:

Elsa Schiaparelli's memoirs, *Shocking Life*, were published simultaneously in 1954 by J. M. Dent & Sons in London, and E. P. Dutton & Co. in New York, as well as in French by Denoël in Paris with the title *Shocking*.

The quotations are taken from the following publications, in the order of their appearance in the text:

Jean Cocteau, "From Worth to Alix," *Harper's Bazaar*, March 1937.

Elsa Schiaparelli, *Shocking Life* (London: J. M. Dent & Sons, 1954).

Virgil Thomson, *Virgil Thomson* (New York: Alfred A. Knopf, 1966), 153.

Madge Garland, *The Indecisive Decade* (London: Macdonald & Co., 1968), 11.

Palmer White, *Elsa Schiaparelli, Empress of Paris Fashion* (London: Aurum Press, 1986), 136.

CLOTHING AND ACCESSORIES

Elsa Schiaparelli by Valérie Belin

Invited by the Musée des Arts Décoratifs, the photographer Valérie Belin interprets a selection of thirty-two items bearing the Schiaparelli label from the museum's collection. The choice reflects a chronological range, from 1928 to 1953, of the clothes and accessories Elsa Schiaparelli donated to the Union Française des Arts du Costume (Ufac). It also takes into account the decorative richness of the outfits, especially the Lesage embroidery, innovative fabrics, and dazzling colors used by the designer. Through her photographs, Belin reveals her encounter with Elsa Schiaparelli's creations and explains her approach:

> As a superb, "shocking," unconventional soul inspired by surrealism, Schiaparelli conceived of her fashion as art. Her clothes decorated a dreamlike world thanks to their narrative effects, often focused on patterns, embroidery, and trompe l'oeil.
>
> By removing any realistic representations or references to a garment's actual use, I wanted to pay homage to the dreaminess and luxurious of this haute couture universe. By accenting the decorative details of each garment rather than its overall shape, I tried to play the fashion artists' narrative game to reproduce a timeless mood and reveal her clothing's poetic vitality. Thus my photographic shifts play on blurriness, low lighting, and color transformations to awaken each piece's dormant symbols.
>
> Thus foliage quivers in a flowing breeze, a motif flutters along a slender silhouette, a blazing inner sun burns passionately or escapes from a place where precious, ready-to-pick cherries, radiant as stained-glass windows, seem to have been precisely drawn by Arcimboldo. Meanwhile embroidered jewels are revealed in accents as they glide gracefully through the fresh, cheerful world of a painter.
>
> V.B.

Valérie Belin is a visual artist and photographer. Her minimal, yet paradoxically baroque-inspired work usually focuses on still lifes and portraits, although dresses, accessories, ornaments, and jewelry also have a special place in her oeuvre. In the 1990s, she photographed wedding dresses by designer Fabien Durand, the dress collections at the Musée des Beaux-Arts et de la Dentelle in Calais, a Christian Lacroix dress, and the Musée des Arts Décoratifs collection for the *Garde-robes* exhibition. In 2000 her noteworthy series of photographs of Moroccan brides in traditional dress was characterized by their monumental, ornamental aspect. Playing on appearances, she took portraits of dummies and real models, then explored the theme of the representation of women in portraits of fictional women in series entitled Modern Royals, China Girls, Painted Ladies, All Star, and Super Models.

SWEATER 1928

Wool knit
Purchased in 2005
Inv. 2005-39-1

In January 1927, the thirty-six-year-old Elsa Schiaparelli presented her first collection of hand-knit sweaters and skirts in her home at 20 rue de l'Université in Paris. Featured in *Vogue Paris* in February, these "sweaters designed specifically for sports" assured her rapid success and fame. These early creations were decorated with the geometric motifs then in fashion and typical of the art deco style: stripes, stepped patterns, rectangles, and trompe l'oeil collars or flapper-style ties. Considered sportswear, these practical, relaxed models could also be worn to high-society events; paired with a wool or crepe de chine skirt, they were accessorized with a belt or costume jewelry.[1] "Convinced deep within me that I was nearly glamourous, I wore it at a smart lunch—and created a furore. . . . All the women wanted one, immediately,"[2] wrote Schiaparelli.

The success of these sweaters was not only due to their artistic originality or ambiguous trompe l'oeil motifs, but also to the uniqueness of the hand stitches; they created a tweed-like surface of wool yarns in contrasting colors "so that it gave an effect reminiscent of the impressionist school of painting"[3] and helped the sweater keep its shape when worn. In her memoirs, Schiaparelli wrote about the evolution of the project[4] and her collaboration with Armenian knitters; her meeting with Aroosiag Mikaëlian, otherwise known as "Mike," who knitted sweaters, caps, scarves, and gloves for her, had a decisive effect on her career.[5]

This renowned black sweater with its large, white trompe l'oeil bow received an enthusiastic welcome in the United States, so much so that *Vogue* called it an "artistic masterpiece" in its December 1927 edition. Schiaparelli's sweaters were widely distributed on the other side of the Atlantic as of fall 1927 by the wholesaler Leonard Davidow, who also sold Sonia Delaunay raincoats.[6] This collaboration revealed the ambitious commercial strategy of the young Parisian entrepreneur and the early support of American businessmen interested in importing avant-garde Parisian styles for a clientele enamored of modernity.

The international success of these early creations meant that the fashion designer could assemble the funds needed in December 1927 to open her "Schiaparelli for sport" salon at 4 rue de la Paix dedicated to sport and leisure clothing. This iconic design with an asymmetrical, trompe l'oeil white and red collar inspired by the neckerchiefs typical of the Deauville region, according to *Harper's Bazaar*,[7] was no doubt presented in January 1928 in Schiaparelli's new location.

From her company's early days, Schiaparelli built her image as an inspired designer by posing for the American photographer Thérèse Bonney wearing the sweater and a cloche hat by Suzanne Talbot (see p. 72).

M.-P.R.

1. Thérèse and Louise Bonney, *A Shopping Guide to Paris* (New York: Robert M. McBride & Company, 1929), 87.
2. Elsa Schiaparelli, *Shocking Life* (London: J. M. Dent & Sons, 1954), 48.
3. Ibid., 49.
4. Ibid., 48.
5. *Hommage à Schiaparelli* (Paris: Musée de la Mode et du Costume, 1984), 121.
6. *Women's Wear Daily*, November 17, 1927, SIII, 14.
7. *Harper's Bazaar*, March 1928, 95.

Thérèse Bonney, *Elsa Schiaparelli*, gelatin silver print, 1928, New York Public Library, inv. 87PH048.1599.

Harper's Bazar, March 1928, p. 95.

WHAT TO WEAR ON BOARD SHIP

The Ideal Costume is Practical, Simple, Dark-Colored, and Designed for Travel and not for Sport

BY MARJORIE HOWARD

15 rue de la Paix, Paris.

I WAS asked to write this article. We were discussing in the New York office my recent crossing on the *Berengaria*, and I had described the clothes of an internationally celebrated member of the smart set, whose name would be recognized by all of you.

"She was such a contrast to some women," I concluded, "who seem to think that a sea voyage is an opportunity to display their most elaborate trappings, entirely forgetting that they are traveling."

"Why don't you write an article about how to dress on shipboard?" they asked me.

"Because Harper's Bazar readers would never commit these solecisms," I answered.

But we all agreed that, even if you are dressed exactly right, there is a subtle satisfaction in reading a confirmation of your judgment. So we decided that, for the March issue, when so many people are beginning to think of reservations and steamer tickets, I might appropriately write about steamer clothes.

Baron de Meyer showed his usual wisdom when he counseled the ocean traveler, in a recent article, to dress as though she never changed her clothes throughout the voyage, in order to be taken for a member of that exclusive Forty, formerly referred to as the Four Hundred. This is the general principle of ship dressing; I can only go into details. Of course, one really has more than one costume; the changes in the weather and the variations in the temperature make that obligatory. But, as they are all in one color scheme, they look the same to the casual observer. The lady I mentioned had chosen navy blue. This is the regular sea color, you know, and has been for generations. There must be some reason for one color in all the naval uniforms of the world. Navy blue is not affected by salt water, neither does it

SCHIAPARELLI

Sweaters are ideal on shipboard; one should have several of them. Schiaparelli makes a new one in fine wool, with the handkerchief knitted as part of it, imitating the popular Deauville mouchoir

APRON
Spring 1935

Rhodophane by Colcombet, crepe de chine, taffeta, and coated canvas
Gift of Elsa Schiaparelli, Ufac, 1973
Inv. UF 73-21-53

This pink apron, originally worn with a midnight-blue dress with low-cut back, made up an outfit that was representative of the daring style Elsa Schiaparelli brought to Paris couture in the mid-1930s. The unusual model, designed for evening, was worn by Mrs. Harrison Williams,[1] the future Mona von Bismarck, and was part of the final collection presented in Schiaparelli's salon at 4 rue de la Paix on October 29, 1934, for spring 1935. Here the designer dared to rework a bib apron, a utilitarian garment cut with a point in front and decorated with a ring of camelias around the neck: "The accent is on the face by framing it softly . . . the objective is to have completely symmetrical lines from head to toe,"[2] declared the house's press release in defining the collection's silhouette.

To balance the clean, uncluttered cut and the play of two contrasting colors, one of her signatures, the designer added a touch of originality by choosing one of the latest technologically innovative textiles. Since the early 1930s, she had intentionally sought out exclusive, synthetic new fabrics, which she claimed were a fundamental characteristic of the Schiaparelli style[3]—rayon crepe with a crinkle "tree bark" effect, wool mixed with feathers,[4] and innovative materials like cellophane. For this, she worked closely with fabric manufacturers such as Ducharne, Bianchini-Férier, and Colcombet. The latter, a Saint Étienne-based company managed by Johan Colcombet at the cutting edge in its use of innovative materials and new manufacturing processes, supplied her with Rhodophane for this apron. The design, photographed by Egidio Scaioni in February 1935, was presented to the press as "Schiaparelli's original glass dress."[5]

Its grooved weave is crossed by narrow, translucent bands that give it a shiny look. The surprising fabric is definitely cellophane.
Cellophane was woven into velvet for a suit or into various transparent fabrics with a surrealist look Schiaparelli used for embroideries or hats. Rhodophane, reinforced by silk or rayon threads,[6] was also used to make a cape and skirt worn over a pale blue satin evening dress, immortalized in *Vogue Paris* by George Hoyningen-Huene.[7]

M.-P.R.

1. Elsa Schiaparelli, "My slightly Shocking life in high fashion," *Maclean's*, October 15, 1954, 106.
2. Press release, October 1934, Maison Schiaparelli.
3. Press release, May 1934, Maison Schiaparelli.
4. "An extraordinary feather wool." Ibid.
5. *L'Officiel de la couture et de la mode*, February 1935, 40.
6. Dilys E. Blum, *Shocking! The Art and Fashion of Elsa Schiaparelli*, exh. cat. (Philadelphia: Philadelphia Museum of Art, 2003), 69.
7. *Vogue Paris*, January 1935, 44.

Egidio Scaioni, *Model Wearing a Elsa Schiaparelli Evening Dress*, photograph, 1935. Palais Galliera, Musée de la Mode de la Ville de Paris, Paris, inv. 2019.2.16

EVENING CAPE
Summer 1935

Simoun crinkle taffeta by Bianchini-Férier
Gift of Elinor Brodie, Ufac, 1969
Inv. UF 69-28-18

In January 1935, Elsa Schiaparelli moved her couture house to more spacious quarters at the Hôtel de Fontpertuis, 21 place Vendôme. This new page in her history was marked by the February 5 presentation of her summer 1935 collection in salons that had been decorated by Jean-Michel Frank. In the over one looks models presented, including this evening cape, the fashion designer proposed creations that were not developed around a specific theme and showed her inventiveness, which by then had captured the public's attention: "Stop, Look, and Listen was the theme of the year. Schiap went up into the rarefied skies of her most fantastic imagination. . . .

Fantasy and ingenuity broke forth, with complete indifference not merely to what people would say but even to what was practical."[1] She imagined a "celestial silhouette"[2] where draped fabrics enveloped the body like saris, showed new "glass" accessories, introduced a fabric featuring her good-luck charm, the Great Bear constellation, dared to use daytime woolens for evening, and, in collaboration with Colcombet, "the most daring of the textile men,"[3] introduced a print made of press clips featuring her image, not unlike cubist collages.

The long, "Venetian" cape worn by Madeline Dittenhofer, one of the designer's American clients, is an innovative, unlined evening model without shoulder pads, simply ties at the neck. It is cut in a crinkle taffeta known as Simoun designed by Bianchini-Férier for which Elsa Schiaparelli had the exclusive rights.[4] As seen in the drawing now in the Musée des Arts Décoratifs, the pink version first presented to clients, journalists, and buyers was paired with a long, navy blue dress with a train whose waist was emphasized by a giant bow. This lightweight cape first appeared in the fall 1934 collection and was subsequently made in a number of variations. For summer 1935, a second, bright green, hooded model worn over a pale pink dress was illustrated by Kees van Dongen for *Harper's Bazaar* (see p. 80) and worn by the American socialite and decorator Lady Mendl. A later version dated 1951 and now in the Musée des Arts Décoratifs[5] is in a fuchsia shot taffeta that resembled Simoun with a voluminous collar that fell sensually on the shoulders.

M.-P.R.

1. Elsa Schiaparelli, *Shocking Life* (London: J. M. Dent & Sons, 1954), 71.
2. Press release, February 1935, Maison Schiaparelli.
3. Schiaparelli, *Shocking*, 74.
4. Dilys E. Blum, *Shocking! The Art and Fashion of Elsa Schiaparelli*, exh. cat. (Philadelphia: Philadelphia Museum of Art, 2003).
5. Musée des Arts Décoratifs, Paris, inv. UF 73-21-20.

Harper's Bazaar, July 1935, p. 26. Drawing by Kees van Dongen.

Design drawing, cape and evening dress, summer 1935 collection. Musée des Arts Décoratifs, Paris, gift of Elsa Schiaparelli, Ufac, 1973, inv. UF-D-73-21-696.

PAIR OF GLOVES
Winter 1936–37

Suede, lace
Gift of Elsa Schiaparelli, Ufac, 1973
Inv. UF 73-21-77 AB

This pair of gloves imitating manicured hands with painted nails was part of the "small details" chapter in the winter 1936–37 collection program[1]—the nails, painted blue veins, and palm lines are depicted in trompe l'oeil. The pair Schiaparelli gave to the Ufac collection are in pink suede and the nails are evoked by openwork black lace. Another variation exists in black suede with red snakeskin nails.[2] These unusual gloves, which create a trompe l'oeil effect down to the fingertips, are in the image of the winter 1936–37 collection that marked the beginning of the fashion designer's collaboration with the artist Salvador Dalí. The Spanish painter attended the collection's presentation in August 1936 with his English friend and sponsor Edward James who also paid for Gala Dalí's couture outfits. *Women's Wear Daily*, the American fashion newspaper, enthusiastically featured the amusing, fantastic surrealist suits, a hit with buyers, on its front page.[3]

The surrealist mood of these gloves was probably inspired by a 1935 Man Ray photograph that shows two gloved hands painted in trompe l'oeil by Picasso[4] (see p. 84). Schiaparelli reversed the visual game: the gloves became strange, animated hands, an unsettling illusion of a second skin.

M.-S.C.C.

1. Maison Schiaparelli. Hortense MacDonald wrote the English version of the introductory text: "Surrealism is applied to dress, after Salvador Dalí." The term "surrealism" disappeared in the French translation: "*Le réalisme d'après Salvador Dalí.*"

2. Philadelphia Museum of Art, Philadelphia, inv. 1969-232-55d,e.

3. *Women's Wear Daily*, August 6, 1936, 1.

4. Dilys E. Blum, *Shocking! The Art and Fashion of Elsa Schiaparelli*, exh. cat. (Philadelphia: Philadelphia Museum of Art, 2003), 131.

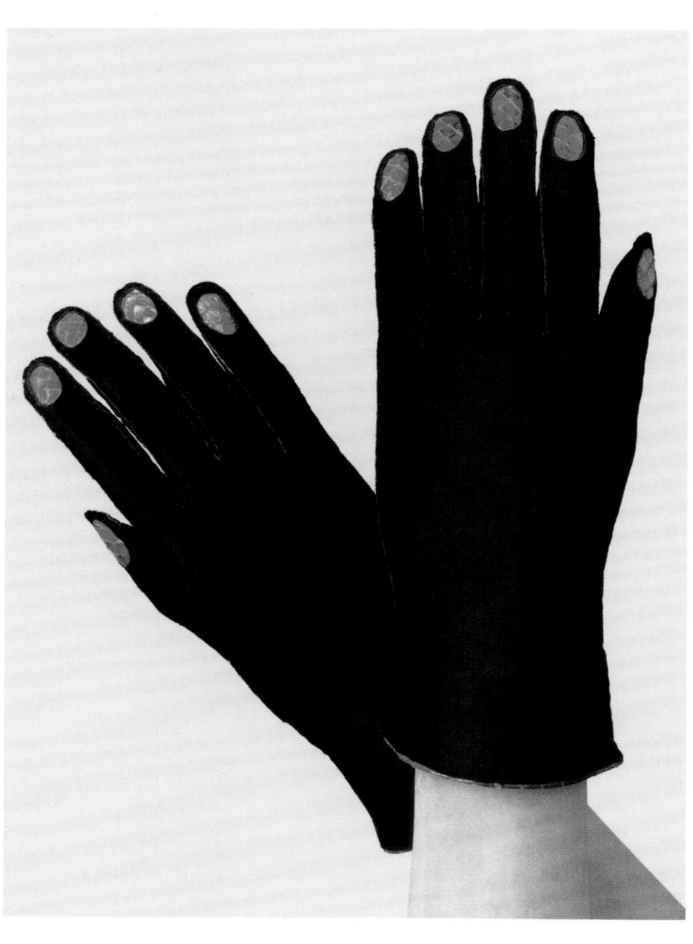

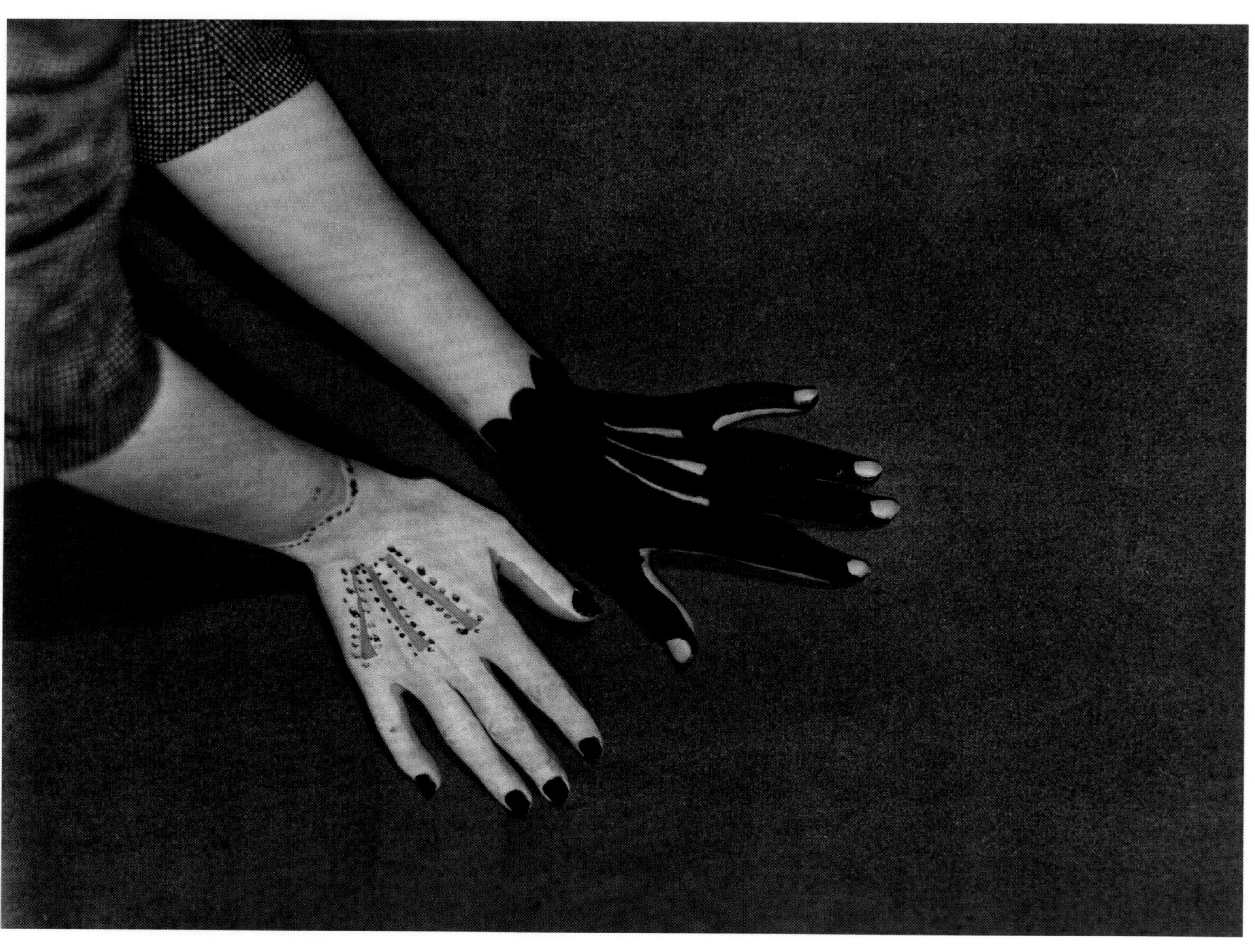

Elsa Schiaparelli, pair of gloves, fall-winter 1937. Philadelphia Museum of Art, Philadelphia, gift of Elsa Schiaparelli, 1969, inv. 1939-232-55d, e.

Man Ray, *Hands Painted by Pablo Picasso*, gelatin silver print, c. 1935. Musée National d'Art Modern – Centre de Création Industrielle, Paris, payment in kind 1994, inv. AM 1994-394 (4248).

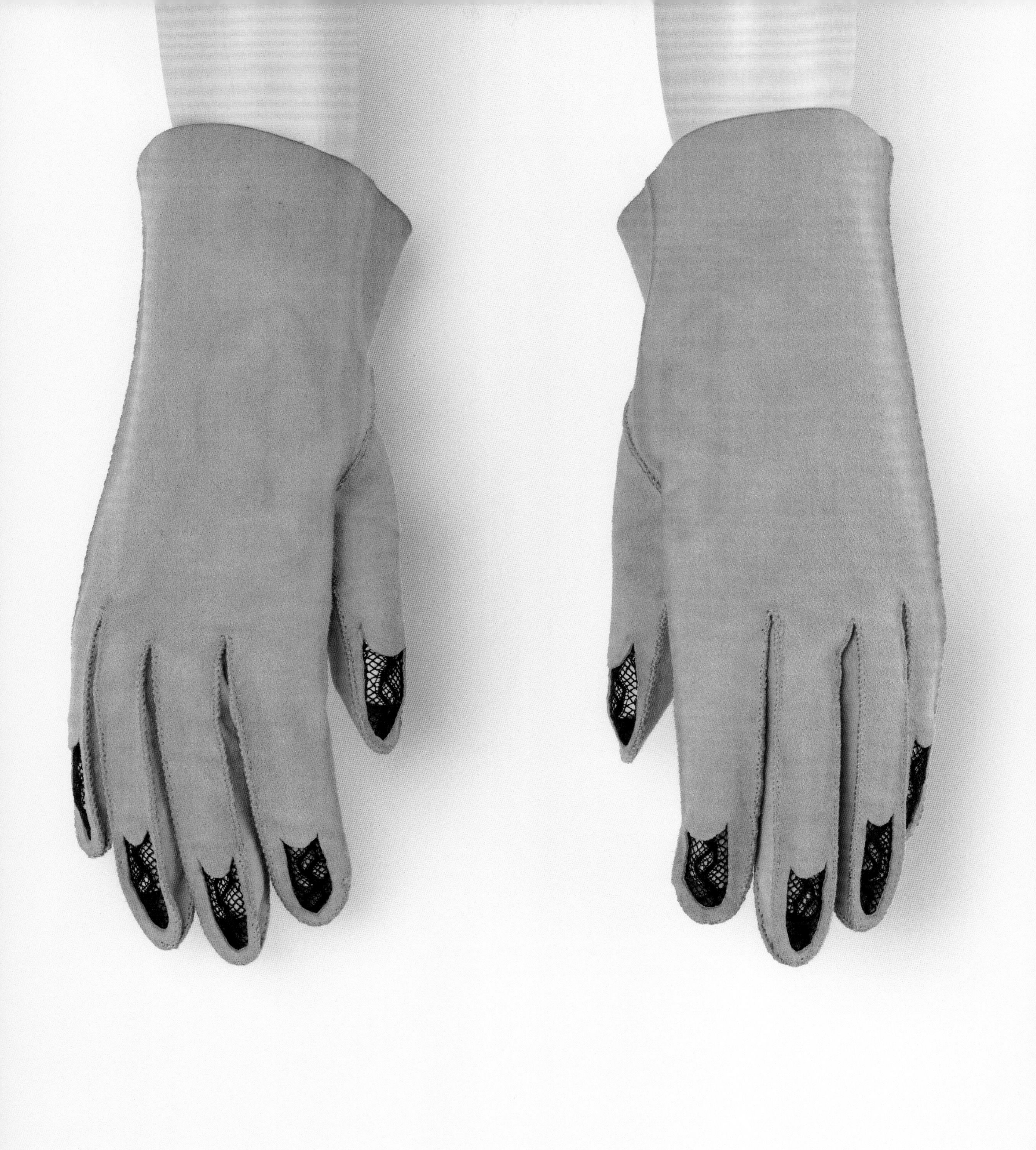

EVENING JACKET
Winter 1936–37

Wool embroidered with lamellae and sequins by Lesage
Gift of Patricia López-Willshaw, Ufac, 1966
Inv. UF 66-38-10

This short, fitted evening jacket in black wool has a silk crepe lining in the same color. All of the embroidery by Lesage was placed at the jacket edges and on its pockets to brighten up its sober, structured lines. From 1936, Schiaparelli worked with Lesage exclusively for all of her embroidery. The jacket, as seen in the design drawing, fastens with gold passementerie buttons, is worn over a black crepe dress and accessorized with a cone-shaped hat covered in glycerinated ostrich feathers.

In 1936 Marlene Dietrich visited Paris to renew her wardrobe and visited her favorite couture houses as reported in *Vogue* magazine. Her first stop was Schiaparelli but she also went to Lanvin, Alix, and Molyneux, not forgetting Madame Agnès and Caroline Reboux for hats.[1] The actress bought this evening jacket embroidered with gold-sequined palm trees during her visit to Schiaparelli's salons. Patricia López-Willshaw, a wealthy Chilean aesthete, also bought this jacket.

The palm tree motif evokes Napoleon Bonaparte's native Corsica as well as his Egyptian campaign. After his victory at Austerlitz, a decision was made in 1806 to build the Vendôme column topped by a bronze sculpture depicting him as a Roman emperor. François Kollar's photograph of Elsa Schiaparelli in front of her salon window looking out to the Vendôme column pays homage to this imperial neighbor. It inspired the painter Étienne Drian, a friend of Schiaparelli, to write a poem entitled "In the shadow of Napoleon": "The capricious Swallow / Who comes to us from Italy / In the shadow of Napoleon / Whistling on her perch / Knows how to construct unusual nests." The fashion designer speaks about this proximity in her memoirs: "The column, one hundred and fifty feet high, on the summit of which Napoleon, dressed like a Roman Caesar, mounts guard, is surrounded by banks, jewellers, and such hotels as the Ritz. Here is undoubtedly the greatest cluster of wealth in Paris."[2] The palm tree motif was certainly inspired by the embroidery on the long, white satin, gold-brocade tunic under the imperial greatcoat immortalized by Jacques-Louis David in his painting *The Coronation of Napoleon*. Designed by the painter Jean-Baptiste Isabey, the richly embroidered coronation outfit can be seen in many official full-length paintings of Napoleon. A similar jacket, a gift from Elsa Schiaparelli, is now in the Philadelphia Museum of Art.[3]

M.-S.C.C.

1. "Dietrich Invades Paris," *Vogue*, November 1936, 134.
2. Elsa Schiaparelli, *Shocking Life* (London: J.M. Dent & Sons, 1954), 70.
3. Philadelphia Museum of Art, Philadelphia, inv. 1969-232-12.

Vogue Paris, October 1936, p. 43. Photograph by André Durst.

Design drawing, jacket and evening dress, winter collection 1936–37. Musée des Arts Décoratifs, Paris, gift of Elsa Schiaparelli, Ufac, 1973, inv. UF-D-73-21-1178.

EVENING JACKET
Summer 1937

Wool, Rhodoid buttons
Gift of Patricia López-Willshaw, Ufac, 1966
Inv. UF 66-38-11

The summer 1937 collection presented on February 4 was devoted to the butterfly, a universal symbol of evanescent beauty and the mysteries of metamorphosis, a subject dear to Elsa Schiaparelli's surrealist friends. Here, the designer became, more than ever, part of the artistic effervescence of 1930s Paris by integrating into her clothing the notions of apparitions and wonder, which "accomplished the miracle of merging with the ordinary and the mundane in the most natural way."[1] Thus butterflies flutter through day and evening designs, are featured in prints, alight on the shoulders of capes, are "trapped" in netting, and flourish on dresses.

This day jacket, worn over a wool dress and with a boater-style straw hat decorated with butterflies, is eloquent: besides her mastery of cut, the designer brings an innovative touch, not only by proposing a collarless jacket similar to a cardigan,[2] but also by amusingly highlighting the front closure with a flurry of painted Rhodoid butterflies placed along the neckline in decreasing sizes. Only the bottom butterfly is a real button and even the oversized buttonholes are simply decorative. Both utilitarian and ornamental, Schiaparelli's buttons are her signature: whimsical, theatrical, and completely unexpected.

This jacket's elegant originality, immortalized in a photograph by Horst P. Horst[3] (see p. 93), was incarnated by two of the house's important clients: socialite Patricia López-Willshaw, a well-known figure in high-society Paris who bequeathed this jacket to Ufac in 1966, and Wallis Simpson, the future Duchess of Windsor, who ordered seventeen pieces from the collection for her summer wardrobe.

M.-P.R.

1. Yves Duplessis, *Le Surréalisme* (Paris: Presses universitaires de France, 1950), 30.
2. *Vogue*, March 15, 1937, 90.
3. Ibid.

Vogue, 15 March 1937, p. 90. Photograph by Horst P. Horst.

Design drawing, evening jacket, winter collection 1936–37. Musée des Arts Décoratifs, Paris, gift of Elsa Schiaparelli, Ufac, 1973, inv. UF-D-73-21-1178.

Design for costume, late nineteenth century, gift of Elsa Schiaparelli, Ufac, 1973.

EVENING DRESS
Summer 1937

Printed silk crepe
Gift of Monsieur Perrigot, Ufac, 1950
Inv. UF 50-17-12

"Schiaparelli's butterflies lend their fantasy and flight to lightweight dresses. They are exotic, colorful, bucolic, and charming."[1] This long, black crepe evening dress is decorated with large reserve-printed butterflies on a white ground. This sleeveless summer model with a low-cut back is closed by a zipper on the left side and has a train. This garment was part of the summer 1937 collection presented in the designer's Place Vendôme couture salons on February 4. The sketch for this model was reproduced in the American magazine Life where it was noted to have been purchased by Wallis Simpson, nicknamed "bride of the year" and the future Duchess of Windsor, for her trousseau. The dress was worn under a coat made of a black crin whose structure, reminiscent of a butterfly net, adds volume to the shoulders.[2] The front page of *Women's Wear Daily* featured a few sketches of the eighteen Schiaparelli garments in Mrs. Simpson's wardrobe.[3]

The stages of the insect's metamorphosis from a caterpillar to a winged butterfly, ephemerally beautiful, fascinated artists, especially the surrealists. In the early 1930s, the American photographer Man Ray, a friend of Elsa Schiaparelli, photographed butterflies with open wings in black and white, and in color (see p. 96). These photographs illustrate the lepidopteran's artistic richness as a still life that one might see in an entomologist's boxed collections. The images were no doubt a source of inspiration for Elsa who knew of the natural transformation of the chrysalis from its gracelessness to a beautiful fluttering insect. Butterflies and moths in black and white or color were some of her many print variations in the summer 1937 collection[4].

M.-S.C.C.

1. *Vogue Paris*, April 1937, 46.
2. "The Bride of the Year," *Life*, May 1937, 64.
3. "Paris radios sketches of Schiaparelli costumes in Mrs. Simpson's wardrobe," *Women's Wear Daily*, April 30, 1937, 1.
4. See also p. 98.

Man Ray, *Butterflies*,
gelatin silver print, c. 1930.
Metropolitan Museum of Art,
New York, inv. 1977.539.

Life, May 17, 1937, p. 64.
Unknown photographer.

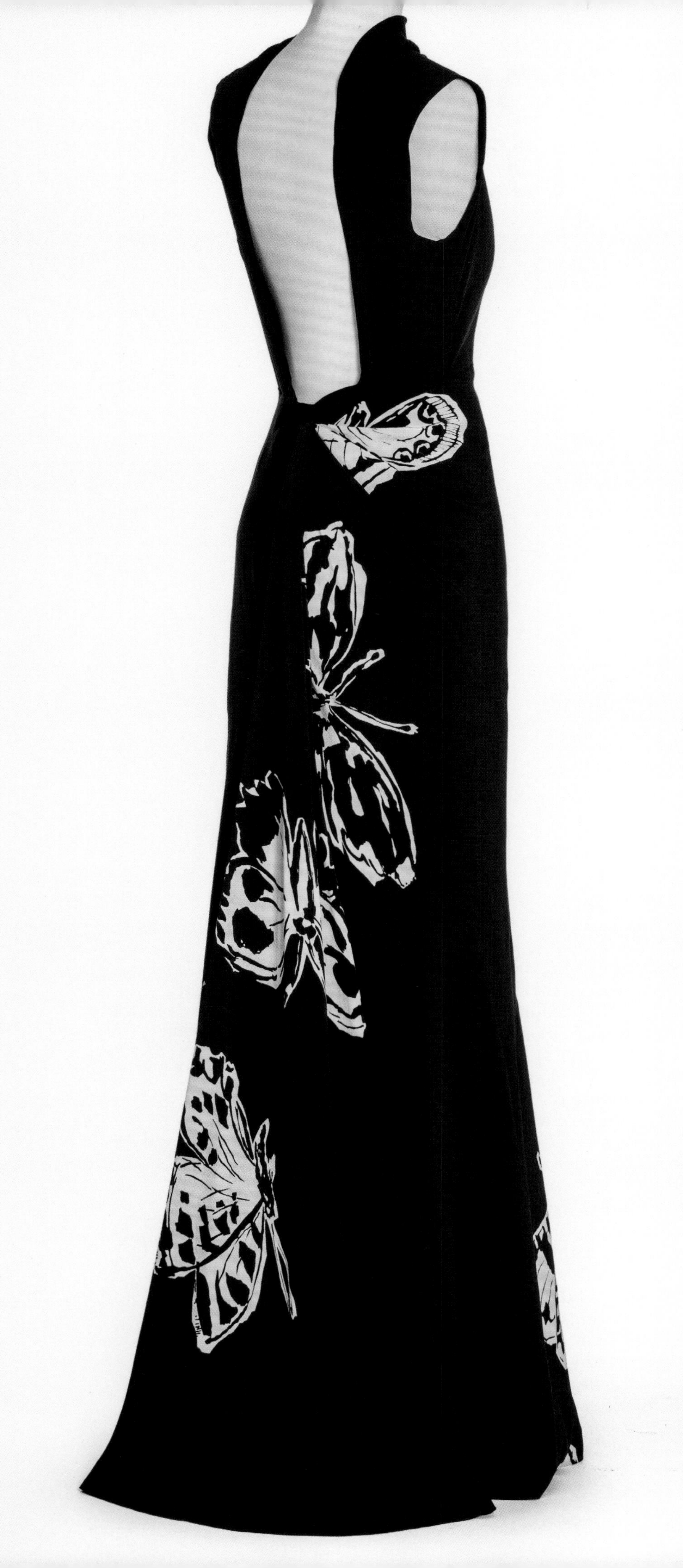

EVENING OUTFIT
Summer 1937

Printed silk satin, silk crepe, filet by Ducharne
Gift of Patricia López-Willshaw, Ufac, 1966
Inv. UF 66-38-4 AB

“What could be more poetic than saying that a woman is a flower and her dress a flower bed? Airy butterflies are the spirit of fashion.”[1] This evening outfit was from the summer 1937 collection presented to individual clients, American buyers, and the press on February 4. The press release, written by Hortense MacDonald, paid homage to each model's joyous movement: “The collection is a farandole . . . A melody wafts from these waltz dresses in lightweight chiffon . . . Singing birds, buzzing bees and cheerful butterflies come together in harmony on summer prints.”[2] This joyous mood was also mentioned in *Women's Wear Daily*: Butterflies flutter throughout the entire Schiaparelli collection, which is more fun and colorful than ever with new outfits and cheerful ideas.[3]

In a photograph by André Durst, Patricia López-Willshaw, one of Schiaparelli's main clients and close friend of the art patron Marie-Laure de Noailles, wears this long silk satin dress printed with multicolored butterflies under a stiff tulle coat made of artificial crin[4] (see p. 100). The illustrator Christian Bérard sketched the silhouette in profile in black ink, which highlighted the coat and transparent effects of the fishnet.[5] The visual effect of the transparent coat with open-weave does not hide the dress but rather envelops it in “a crisp cloud of raw color.”[6] *Vogue* magazine describes the charm of hunting butterflies evoked by the ensemble: “The dress underneath seems captured in the snares of a net, the brilliant butterfly has finally been caught.”[7] For Wallis Simpson, another loyal client, the black tulle coat with a black, butterfly-shaped belt clasp also covered the white butterfly-printed evening dress like a butterfly net.[8]

M.-S.C.C.

1. *Vogue Paris*, March 1937, 29.
2. Press release, Maison Schiaparelli.
3. *Women's Wear Daily*, February 4, 1937, 1.
4. *Vogue Paris*, July 1937, 23.
5. *Vogue*, April 1937, 70.
6. *Vogue*, March 1937, 29.
7. *Vogue*, March 1937, 66.
8. Musée des Arts Décoratifs, Paris, inv. UF 50-17-12

ANDRÉ DURST

MARCEL ROCHAS

LA PRINCESSE C. TROUBETZKOÏ

SCHIAPARELI

MADAME A. LOPEZ-WINNSHAW

LA PRINCESSE KARAM DE KAPURTHALA

MAINBOCHER

FLEURS ET PAPILLONS

23

Vogue Paris, July 1937, p. 23. Photograph by André Durst.

Design drawing, evening ensemble, summer 1937 collection. Musée des Arts Décoratifs, Paris, gift of Elsa Schiaparelli, Ufac, 1973, inv. UF-D-73-21-1553.

EVENING JACKET
Spring 1938

Silk velvet, embroidered with lamellae, cannetilles, and claw-set stones by Lesage, molded resin buttons with flowers
Gift of Elsa Schiaparelli, Ufac, 1973
Inv. UF 73-21-68

This evening jacket in violet silk velvet lined in a matching silk crepe is fastened by five transparent resin buttons with tiny, bright pink flowers. Textured, botanical embroidery by Maison Lesage livens up the front of the jacket and forms the pockets. Baroque flowers, made with gold-plated lamellae accented by tiny ruby mirrors, give the embroidery more texture and shading.

Albert Lesage, director of his company's workshop, collaborated closely with Schiaparelli to create innovative embroideries. He brought back the cannetille, a twisted metallic thread. He used metal to outline diverse uses and introduced, at Schiaparelli's request, special materials from modern industry such as plastic. The evening jacket Schiaparelli perfected in different collections, beginning in the mid-1930s, was much appreciated by her clients for restaurant dinners, concerts, and high-society receptions. According to Bettina Ballard, Paris correspondent for American *Vogue*, "Night racing at Longchamp, for example, looked like the opening of a Schiaparelli collection."[1] This fitted jacket, decorated with embroidery, could be taken off during the evening to reveal a long dress, cut low in the back, as seen in the corresponding sketch[2] (see p. 105). Schiaparelli was the first to use buttons as spectacular decorative elements. Featured on *Time* magazine's cover, the caption summed up her role: "Mme Elsa Schiaparelli . . . glorifies the gadget and persecutes the button."[3]

A variation on this jacket, in green silk velvet, is now in New York's Metropolitan Museum of Art[4]. It bears the label of Saks Fifth Avenue, the New York department store that sold Schiaparelli's creations since by then she had developed an international reputation: "Salon Moderne, Saks Fifth Avenue."

M.-S.C.C.

1. Bettina Ballard, *In My Fashion* (London: Secker & Warburg, 1960), 69.
2. Musée des Arts Décoratifs, Paris, inv. UF D 73-21-1652.
3. *Time*, August 13, 1934.
4. Metropolitan Museum of Art, New York, inv. 1978.288.19ac.

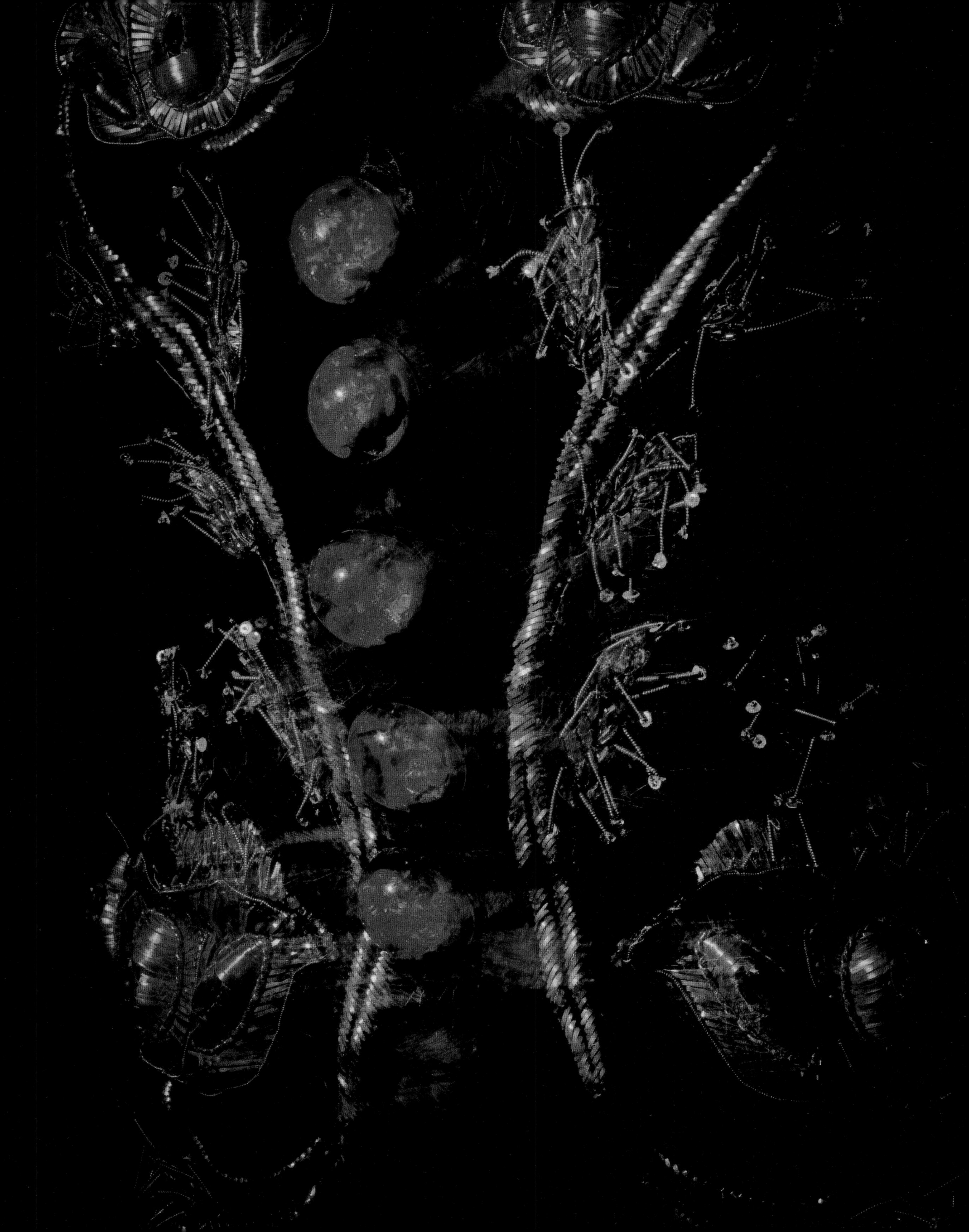

Unknown photographer, *Model Wearing a Schiaparelli Jacket*, photograph, c. 1937.

Design drawing, jacket and evening dress, spring 1938 collection. Musée des Arts Décoratifs, Paris, gift of Elsa Schiaparelli, Ufac, 1973, inv. UF D 73-21-1652.

EVENING BOLERO
Summer 1938

Silk braid embroidery on silk crepe, embroidered with silk thread, ties, cabochons, beads, and mirrors by Lesage
Gift of Elsa Schiaparelli to Ufac, 1973
Inv. UF 73-21-48

This short-sleeved evening bolero, sumptuously embroidered by Lesage with trained elephants and acrobats swinging on tightropes against a background of arabesques, is from the summer 1938 collection with its circus theme. The introduction of the press release given to clients, press and guests on February 4, 1938, at the Place Vendôme salons[1] announced a comedy performance that would include the Fratellini clown trio: A circus at the Place des Fêtes—elephants, apples, caramels—Punchinello in his multicolored costume laughingly blurts out: "Why be serious about something so insignificant and ephemeral as a summer dress?"[2] This evening bolero, as well as the model with prancing horses,[3] were both mentioned in a text by Hortense MacDonald, communications director of the House of Schiaparelli: "You can dazzle for evening by wearing a shiny satin bolero with elephants or prancing horse embroideries over a simple dinner dress." The American publication *Women's Wear Daily*, geared to clothing industry and fashion professionals, described the collection as a "ray of sunshine" that brings joie de vivre.[4] "The most riotous and swaggering collection" had a wild success, remembered the designer in 1954.[5] François Lesage recounted a society event that showed the extent of this craze: "At an Opera charity gala during the summer of 1938, seventeen women seated in the orchestra realized at intermission that they were wearing the same bolero with elephants and prancing horses."[6] In her memoirs, Elsa Schiaparelli remembers the burst of enthusiasm of the fashion show guests: "As an amazing fact, Schiap did not lose a single one of her wealthy conservative old-fashioned clients but got a lot of new ones—and, of course, all the stars."[7] Nicknamed "Madame Avant-Garde" and a great client of Schiaparelli's, Helena Rubinstein, the founder of her own beauty empire, bought this bolero and had herself photographed wearing it with multiple strings of pearls by Boris Lipnitzki[8] (see p. 109).

M.-S.C.C.

1. Maison Schiaparelli.
2. *Women's Wear Daily*, February 15, 1938, 5.
3. Musée des Arts Décoratifs, Paris, inv. UF 73-21-50.
4. *Women's Wear Daily*, February 15, 1938, 5.
5. Elsa Schiaparelli, *Shocking Life* (London: J. M. Dent & Sons, 1954), 99.
6. "Broder pour Schiap, conversation avec François Lesage," *Hommage à Elsa Schiaparelli*, exh. cat. (Paris: Musée de la Mode et du Costume, 1984).
7. Schiaparelli, *Shocking Life*, 99.
8. Marie-Sophie Carron de la Carrière, "Helena Rubinstein et la mode," *Helena Rubinstein, l'aventure de la beauté*, exh. cat (Paris: Flammarion, 2019), 117.

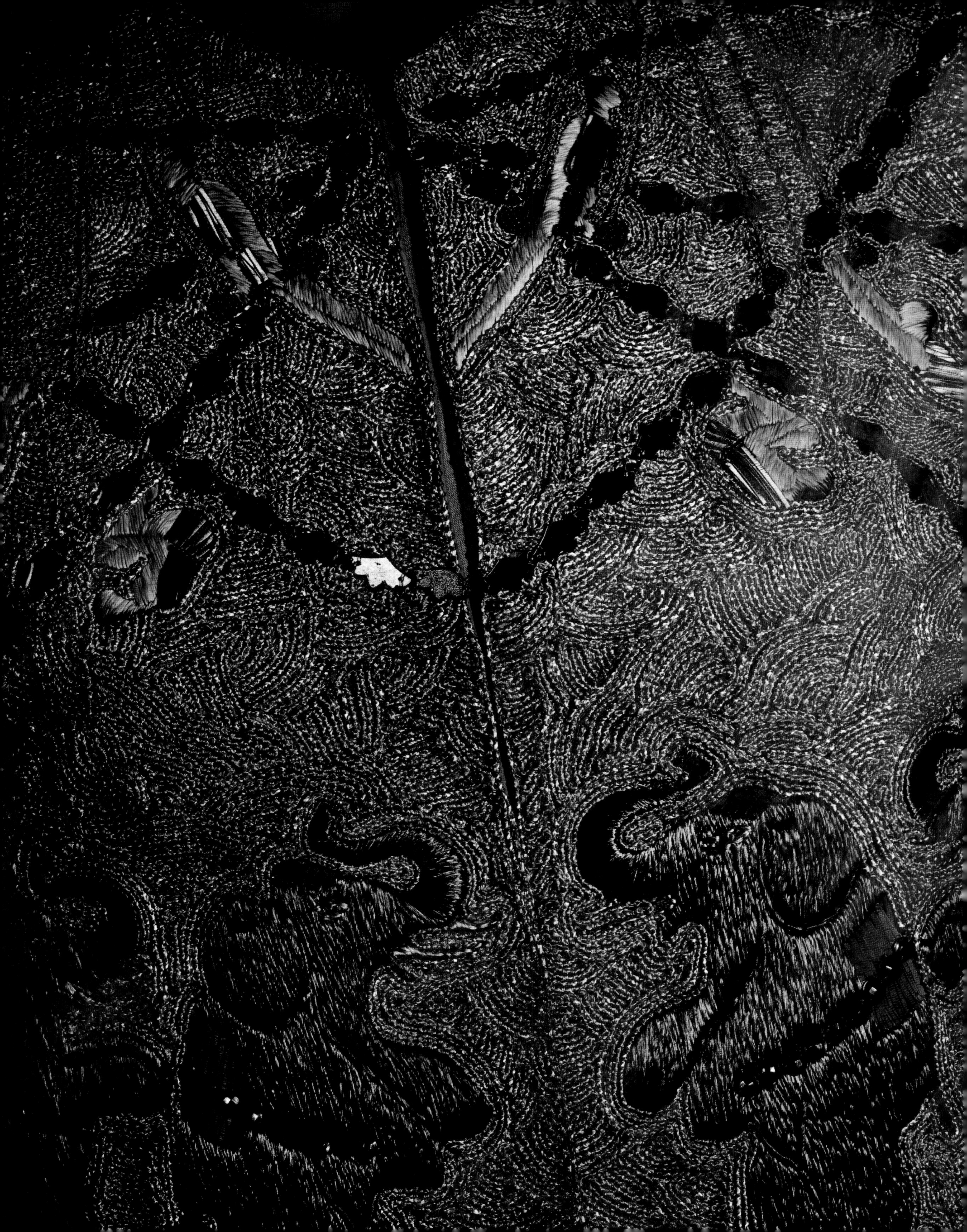

Jean Schlumberger, necklace, 1938, gold-plated metal, glass beads. Musée des Arts Décoratifs, Paris, anonymous gift, 1996, inv. 996.66.7.

Boris Lipnitzki, *Helena Rubinstein Wears Embroidered Bolero by Schiaparelli*, photograph, c. 1938.

EVENING BOLERO
Summer 1938

Silk satin, passementerie, flattened, appliqué ties, silk chenille, lamella, rhinestone, and sequin embroidery by Lesage
Gift of Elsa Schiaparelli, Ufac, 1973
Inv. UF 73-21-50

Sketched by Christian Bérard for *Vogue* magazine,[1] this bolero was part of the summer 1938 Circus collection. The illustrator's comment evokes the unusual mood: "The cheerfulness of the circus inspired Schiaparelli with its motifs, shapes, colors and glitter." This brightly colored, embroidered evening bolero was worn over a long black dress as illustrated in the sketch. The name usually given to this garment, "Prancing horses," evokes trained circus horses. In the 1930s, the Circus d'Hiver in Paris, run by the four Bouglione brothers, was known for its equestrian numbers in the ring, especially the groups of prancing, elegantly dressed horses who had been trained to stand on their hind legs like the ones embroidered on the front of the bolero. Maison Lesage's metallic, glittery embroidery reproduces the vividly colored horse ornaments and plays of light in the ring.

The collection's presentation in the couture salons of 21 place Vendôme was truly a circus spectacle. In her memoirs, Elsa Schiaparelli recalls the extraordinary excitement that reigned: "The most riotous, swaggering collection was that of the circus. Barnum, Bailey, Grock, and the Frattelinis got loose in a mad dance in the dignified showrooms, up and down the imposing staircase, in and out of the windows. Clowns, elephants, horses, decorated the prints with the words 'Attention à la peinture.'"[2]

With this show Schiaparelli launched a circus fashion, a theme that was used by her client Lady Mendl for the costume ball she organized the following July in her Villa Trianon at Versailles that featured circus animals. The hostess appeared as the liontamer "and walked herself between the legs of the elephants. She was draped in a long, floating cape of shocking pink [from the fall 1935 collection] and brandished a whip as if to defy the fates."[3] Schiaparelli, a great fan of costume balls, danced until five o'clock in the morning.

M.-S.C.C.

1. *Vogue*, April 1938, 90–91.
2. Elsa Schiaparelli, *Shocking Life* (London: J. M. Dent & Sons, 1954), 99.
3. Schiaparelli, *Shocking Life*, 110.

Design drawing, bolero and evening dress, summer 1938 collection. Musée des Arts Décoratifs, Paris, gift of Elsa Schiaparelli, Ufac, 1973, inv. UF D 73-21-1862.

Jean Schlumberger, comb, gilt and enameled metal, 1938. Musée des Arts Décoratifs, Paris, anonymous gift, 1996, inv. 996.65.4.5.

Vogue, April 1938, 90-91. Drawings by Christian Bérard.

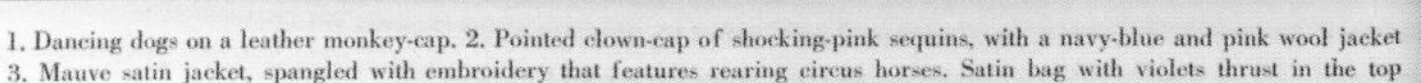

1. Dancing dogs on a leather monkey-cap. 2. Pointed clown-cap of shocking-pink sequins, with a navy-blue and pink wool jacket 3. Mauve satin jacket, spangled with embroidery that features rearing circus horses. Satin bag with violets thrust in the top

4. Tight-rope walker's satin bodice, all glitter and fringe, over a jersey skirt. Fingerless satin gloves with gum-drop buttons 5. Ringmaster's squashed top-hat of felt; plaid suit. 6. More horses on a satin jacket. Crêpe dress; circus-queen ostrich tower

JACKET
Fall 1938

Rayon crepe, moiré, painted metal insects by Jean Schlumberger
Gift of Elsa Schiaparelli, Ufac, 1973
Inv. UF 73-21-70

"This is a Pagan collection,"[1] declared the Maison Schiaparelli press release for the April 28, 1938 presentation of the new fall collection. The couturiere designed over eighty items, most of which resonated with this new theatrical theme tinged with mythological, sylvan, and botanical references inspired by the Florentine Renaissance. The collection was also an opportunity for the designer to reinterpret one of her favorite themes: metamorphosis. Her profound interest in the founding myths of Ovid's *Metamorphoses*, which she had explored as early as 1911 in the book of poems *Arethusa* that paid homage to the nymph who had been transformed into a fountain, opened the way to the fantastical. Thus, her most adventurous clients were transformed into surreal apparitions, illustrating once again "the feeling of the marvelous in the everyday,"[2] as the surrealists saw it.

According to the drawing in the Musée des Arts Décoratifs, this day jacket worn over a dress and topped off by a small, 23-centimeter wide hat,[3] synthesizes the vision presented in the collection: made in a rayon crepe that evokes the rough surface of tree bark, it is structured by two silk velvet braids that, thanks to their clever cut, hide two front pockets. The leaf-shaped black resin buttons were a recurring motif in the collection that the designer developed in various necklaces, belts, textured embroidery, and fabrics. A dissonant detail, the tiny jeweled, painted metal insects that seem to crawl over the flesh pink lapels were the work of Jean Schlumberger who collaborated with Elsa Schiaparelli between 1937 and 1939, and also produced, during the same period, similar vegetable and insect jewelry for the creations of milliner Madame Suzy. We also find them attached to a famous necklace in transparent Rhodoid[4] and, as a common thread, they were placed on hats or transformed into buttons and belt buckles.

Another example of this jacket, now in the Metropolitan Museum of Art in New York, was worn by Millicent Rogers, a rich American heiress known for her daring fashion look who was part of café society and a regular Schiaparelli client.

M.-P.R.

1. Press release, April 1938, Maison Schiaparelli.

2. Françoise Py, "Le surréalisme et les metamorphoses : pour une mythologie moderne," *Mélusine 26* (2006): 10.

3. Dilys E. Blum, *Shocking! The Art and Fashion of Elsa Schiaparelli*, exh. cat. (Philadelphia: Philadelphia Museum of Art, 2003), 185.

4. Two examples of this necklace are in the Metropolitan Museum, New York, inv. 2018.752 and inv. 2009.300.1234.

Harper's Bazaar, June 1938, p. 22. Photograph by George Hoyningen-Huene.

Jean Schlumberger, decorative elements for the hat for the milliner Madame Suzy, enameled gilt metal, c. 1938. Musée des Arts Décoratifs, Paris, anonymous gift, 1996, inv. 996.65.2.11 to 18.

EVENING CAPE
Fall 1938

Silk organdy, goffered silk taffeta, glass tube bead embroidery
Gift of Patricia López-Willshaw, Ufac, 1966
Inv. UF 66-38-14

This cape, worn over a long, narrow, fluid dress, is one of the most iconic, radical pieces in the Pagan collection of fall 1938. Elsa Schiaparelli drew inspiration from mythological figures bequeathed to us from antiquity, an endless source of inspiration for artists during the Renaissance and subsequent centuries that also interested the surrealists. The designer helped update these myths in her creations but also created a troubling game of appearances in this unusual couture garment similar in form to a costume. This lightweight evening cape, as "fragile as gossamer wings,"[1] is made of multiple cut-out silk leaves arranged in shades of green like an "artist's palette"[2] and individually sewn onto gauze while the "stem" dress is embroidered with tiny black transparent tube beads that must have shimmered under the bright lights of high-society soirées. Here the myth behind the metamorphosis is at the core of the designer's approach. Schiaparelli transforms the model or client into a fabulous creature: a half-tree, half-human chimera with a surprising appearance. The designer once again drew inspiration from Ovid's *Metamorphoses*, especially the myth of Philemon and Baucis where Daphne is transformed into a laurel tree: "a thin bark closed around her gentle bosom, and her hair became as moving leaves; her arms were changed to waving branches, and her active feet as clinging roots were fastened to the ground—her face was hidden with encircling leaves."[3] Another outfit is also significant: a jacket and evening dress ensemble[4] entirely printed with a motif that evoked the rings of a tree trunk, worn with a hat formed by a tuft of leaves imitating foliage.

These clothes, with their rich literary connotations, define Schiaparelli's interpretation of pagan beauty. However, beyond this observation, her creations were intended to not just be simple couture garments but rather intellectual works that occupied a special place in surrealist iconography.

M.-P.R.

1. Press release, April 1938, Maison Schiaparelli.
2. Ibid.
3. Ovid, *Metamorphoses*, trans. Brookes More (Boston: Cornhill Publishing Co., 1922).
4. Drawing now in the Musée des Arts Décoratifs, inv. UF D-73-21-1829. The jacket and dress outfit are now in the Goldstein Museum of Design, Falcon Heights, Minnesota.

Jean Clément, *Foliage* necklace, gold-plated metal on fabric mount, spring 1938 collection. Musée des Arts Décoratifs, Paris, gift of Barbara Berger, 2004, inv. 2004.160.1.

Design drawing, cape and evening dress, fall 1938 collection. Musée des Arts Décoratifs, Paris, gift of Elsa Schiaparelli, Ufac, 1973, inv. UF-D-73-21-2359.

EVENING DRESS
Fall 1938

Silk crepe, silk and metallic thread embroidery by Lesage, appliqué flower and leaf garlands in coated canvas
Gift of Elsa Schiaparelli, Ufac, 1973
Inv. UF 73-21-7

The fall 1938 Pagan collection included some of the designer's most remarkable creations inspired by Roman mythology. Nurtured by these works, which she had admired while growing up in Rome, Italian art was not a new source of inspiration for Elsa Schiaparelli. In the summer of 1935, she had already proposed long "Venetian" hooded capes and veiled dress ensembles that covered the hair, reminiscent of young aristocratic beauties or the Madonnas painted by the Italian masters. This was similar to a room divider depicting a Virgin with pageboys that she commissioned from Christian Bérard for her Rue Barbet-de-Jouy apartment in 1934 (see p. 60).

In 1938 Schiaparelli once again suggested that her clients incarnate mythical figures by creating ensembles that evoked that imaginary world, such as this evening dress. Typical of the season's line, the dress is svelte and slender like a "flexible reed."[1] The silk cloth shapes the hips and the draped bodice opens to a décolleté embellished with realistically embroidered flower branches and foliage by Maison Lesage. The reference to Florentine culture is seen in her choice of colors for this dress whose violet hue evokes the iris, the emblematic flower of the Tuscan city. The couture was inspired by the dresses and flowered necklaces Sandro Botticelli used when depicting his goddesses and nymphs in *Primavera* and especially *The Birth of Venus*, which she probably saw in the summer of 1935 at the Petit Palais exhibition of Italian art. "Women looked as if they had come out of a Botticelli painting,"[2] she wrote about this collection; an idea she literally brought to life a few years earlier in the summer of 1935, when she made the spectacular Venus costume, working with the hairdresser Antoine, that Vicomtesse Benoist d'Azy wore to Comte Étienne de Beaumont's costume ball with its "famous painting" theme.

Schiaparelli thus transposed the vitality of these masterpieces, lauded by the American art historian and Italian Renaissance specialist Bernard Berenson, into couture: "Look, for instance, at Botticelli's 'Venus Rising from the Sea'. Throughout, the tactile imagination is roused to a keen activity, by itself almost as life-heightening as music."[3]

M.-P.R.

1. Press release, fall 1938, Maison Schiaparelli.
2. Elsa Schiaparelli, *Shocking Life* (London: J. M. Dent & Sons, 1954), 99.
3. Bernard Berenson, *The Italian Painters of the Renaissance* (London: Phaidon Press, 1952), 67.

Vogue Paris, August 1938, p. 34. Anonymous photograph.

Design drawing, evening dress, fall 1938 collection. Musée des Arts Décoratifs, Paris, gift of Elsa Schiaparelli, Ufac, 1973, inv. UF-D-73-21-1953.

EVENING DRESS
Winter 1938–39

Ducharne pekin silk
Gift of Patricia López-Willshaw, Ufac, 1966
Inv. UF 66-38-3

Presented on August 4, 1938, the collection for the following winter was one of Elsa Schiaparelli's most famous since, by the late 1930s, her inspiration and ingenuity had attained its peak. Commonly referred to as the Astrological or Zodiac collection, the theme was built around an evocation of the esoteric mysteries of the constellations, the cosmos, stars (in homage to her uncle Giovanni Schiaparelli, a famous astronomer and director of the Milan observatory), and, by extension the sun, the key symbol of the reign of Louis XIV. The use of a unifying theme was helpful as a communication strategy with journalists and buyers but did not include every creation in the collection, such as this dress.

This evening creation, of which there was no other variation in the collection, is cut in an unusual pekin silk from Ducharne; the movement of its slender line was accentuated in the back by a short train, cut on the bias like an isosceles triangle, that protruded midway down the skirt. The cuts were established by following strict proportions, as Hortense MacDonald explained in *Women's Wear Daily*,[1] specifying that the collection was developed by using *Elements*, Euclid's treatise on geometry and mathematics—"The silhouette is constructed with precise dimensions, the slightest change could destroy the silhouette"[2]—also notes the press release. The historical appeal of this dress, "not strictly 1890 but reminiscent of it"[3] according to *Harper's Bazaar*, is also defined by the two elaborate short balloon sleeves that accentuate the broad shoulders while slimming the waist and hips. A plastic zipper from the Éclair brand, which Schiaparelli was the first to use on evening dresses, runs down the back as a signature reminder of her style.

Contrasting colors, very much in fashion that year,[4] emphasized a fuchsia derived from her favorite color launched in 1937, the famous shocking pink. Her thoughts on color, which that gave her "ecstatic pleasure"[5] and that she used "with the boldness of Picasso"[6] were updated for each collection; the Schiaparelli palette often stands out for the use of bright tones, in the image of her lipstick collection sold in the Schiap boutique and nail polishes, such as those by the American brand Cutex whose advertisements featured a woman wearing this dress.[7]

M.-P.R.

1. *Women's Wear Daily*, August 10, 1938.
2. Press release, August 1938, Maison Schiaparelli.
3. *Harper's Bazaar*, September 1, 1938, 83.
4. *Paris-couture-années trente*, ed. Guillaume Garnier (Paris: Musée de la Mode et du Costume, 1987), 238.
5. Elsa Schiaparelli, *Shocking Life* (London: J.M. Dent & Sons, 1954), 226.
6. Bettina Ballard, *In My Fashion* (London: Secker & Warburg, 1960), 69.
7. *Harper's Bazaar*, November 1938, 149.

Harper's Bazaar, 1st September 1938, p. 83. Photograph by George Hoyningen-Huene.

Design drawing, evening dress, winter 1938–39 collection. Musée des Arts Décoratifs, Paris, gift of Elsa Schiaparelli, Ufac, 1973, inv. UF-D-73-21-2047.

EVENING COAT
Winter 1938–39

Wool, silk velvet, silk taffeta, lamella, sequin, and porcelain flower embroidery by Lesage, resin buttons
Gift of Patricia López-Willshaw, Ufac, 1966
Inv. UF 66-38-6

A faithful client of Elsa Schiaparelli's creations from 1937, Patricia López-Willshaw was the wife of Arturo López-Willshaw, a rich Chilean art collector. After moving in 1928 to the Hôtel Rodocanachi in Neuilly-sur-Seine, just outside Paris, the couple gave splendid parties in their home where they invited everyone who was anyone in Paris. Her extremely confident taste meant that she selected the most spectacular outfits by the Italian designer, which gave her a singular look. Thus, *Vogue* magazine spoke of her "personal choice . . . the indication of true elegance."[1]

The six decorative pockets on the long black wool coat are especially striking. The Lesage embroidery of white, pink, and gold porcelain flowers, and metal lame resemble flowers spread over pink velvet cut in the shape of flowerpots. The textured compositions recall refined, colorful rococo ornaments as well as the exquisite porcelain produced at the Manufacture Royale de Sèvres during the eighteenth century. Intended for a female clientele, pale pink porcelain was a favorite of Versailles courtiers, including Madame de Pompadour, a confidante of Louis XV, who played a key role in his popularity. Since the color was one of the most difficult to obtain because of its instability during firing, its manufacturing represented a technical prowess that contributed to its value. For Schiaparelli, associating pink with the decorative floral embroidery transposes the motifs of her Shocking perfume, whose bottle was a thrilling evocation of femininity.

Another example of this evening coat, a gift of Elsa Schiaparelli in 1969, is now in the Philadelphia Museum of Art.[2] The coat is topped by a headdress, featured in the sketch in the Musée des Arts Décoratifs[3] and visible in a photograph by Constantin Joffé that appeared in *Femina* magazine.[4] Entitled "the Queen Victoria bonnet" in keeping with royal terminology, the headdress "was launched by Schiaparelli as an early evening piece. It is made of a delicately embroidered satin band finished in back by a gathered, black lace veil. The large bow under the chin gives it a special cachet."

M.-S.C.C.

1. *Vogue*, February 1939, 20.
2. Philadelphia Museum of Art, Philadelphia, inv. 1969-32-6.
3. Musée des Arts Décoratifs, Paris, inv. UF D 73-21-2049 bis.
4. *Femina*, September 1938, 40.

Design drawing, evening coat, winter 1937–38 collection. Musée des Arts Décoratifs, Paris, gift of Elsa Schiaparelli, Ufac, 1973, inv. UF-D-73-21-2049 bis.

Vase with rocaille decoration, soft-paste porcelain, 1757–58. Musée National des Châteaux de Versailles et de Trianon, Versailles, inv. V.2018.47.

PHOEBUS EVENING CAPE
Winter 1938–39

Ratteen, quilted silk crepe, paillette, tinsel, and gold thread embroidery by Lesage, passementerie buttons
Gift of Elsa Schiaparelli, Ufac, 1973
Inv. UF 73-21-39

Dramatically sketched by illustrator Christian Bérard in the November 1938 issue of *Vogue*,[1] the short Phoebus cape's mesmerizing back is covered by a radiant golden sun embroidered by Lesage on a shocking pink ground. This broad-shouldered garment is one of the masterpieces in the Zodiac collection that Elsa Schiaparelli presented in her couture salon at 21 place Vendôme on August 4, 1938. There are two identical versions of this cape in France's public collections: one at the Palais Galliera that belonged to Daisy Fellowes and the other at the Musée des Arts Décoratifs, a generous gift from the designer.

The face of Medusa with a petrifying gaze surrounded by hair in the form of luminous rays is at the center of the embroidery. In Lesage's masterful work, the gorgon with a monstrous head is transformed into a lively, almost endearing, even protective image. Evoking a taste for antiquity, the cape, known as Phoebus thanks to its dazzling imagery, is often used as an epithet associated with Apollo, the protective god of all the arts and symbol of the sun and civilizing enlightenment. He specifically incarnates the figure of Louis XIV who made Versailles his sun palace and the home of Apollo from where he spread his beneficial influence around the world. According to a vision that came from antiquity, Schiaparelli made multiple references to Versailles in her winter 1938–39 collection by associating the seasons, the elements, and the planets in a harmonious, grandiose relationship. In the same collection was a black velvet cape decorated on the front with a spectacular gold embroidery that represented the Neptune basin at Versailles. The Neptune cape, a counterpoint to the Phoebus cape, was worn with panache by Schiaparelli's decorator friend Elsie de Wolfe who eventually became Lady Charles Mendl and was photographed by Cecil Beaton in her Versailles home near the chateau. Bequeathed by Lady Mendl's descendants, this garment is now in the Metropolitan Museum of Art in New York.[2]

M.-S.C.C.

1. Christian Bérard, drawing published to illustrate the article "Poufs et pirouettes," *Vogue*, November 1938, 41.
2. Metropolitan Museum of Art, New York, inv. C.I.51.83.

Cecil Beaton, *Lady Mendl wearing the Neptune cape from the winter collection 1938–39*, photograph, c. 1937.

Vogue, 15 October 1938, p. 58. Illustration by Christian Bérard.

EVENING DRESS
Summer 1939

Ducharne printed satin, drawing by Jean Peltier
Purchase made with the support of Susan Bloomberg, 2018
Inv. 2018-65-1

Presented in the Place Vendôme salon on February 6, 1939, this evening dress in white silk satin from the Lyon silkmaker Ducharne was part of the summer collection. It has double straps, a low-cut back and a skirt whose fullness is thrown backwards, accentuating the hips and slim waist. *Vogue* magazine described the collection, which looked back to 1880s fashions: "A fond memory of our grandmothers' bustles at Schiaparelli. Not a real bustle with a horsehair cushion but an amusing reminder of it with giant folds in the back of the skirt."[1] This "look backwards," as the article mentions, had its source in a collection of nineteenth-century fashion engravings that Elsa Schiaparelli gave to Ufac when she donated her clothes and collection drawings. The nineteenth-century *Journal des demoiselles*, intended to educate young, upper class girls, was a favorite source of inspiration for the couture designer who owned some of these engravings.

The bustle dresses from the summer 1939 collection were photographed during a costume ball that year celebrating the fiftieth anniversary of the Eiffel Tower. The cheerful border print designed by Jean Peltier was entitled "women with poodles." It depicts a fashion show of women, seen in profile, wearing hats and dressed in colorful, early Belle Époque ensembles with defined waists and bell-shaped skirts. The inspiration for these women is perhaps Marcel Vertès's drawing of Mae West holding her dog on a leash in the film *Every Day's a Holiday* that was featured in *Harper's Bazaar*.[2] The sketch of the evening dress[3] shows the model with a huge, ostrich-feathered hat resembling the one worn by West. The movie costume made for the star, who was dressed on screen by Elsa Schiaparelli, was the inspiration for the couture piece. The Philadelphia Museum of Art[4] has the same model of this evening dress, a gift from the designer.

The conclusion of the Schiaparelli press release insisted on the optimistic character of the collection in a context of great international tension: "The cheerfulness of new prints, the wide satin and velvet stripes . . . seem to indicate that, after all, things are not so bad and that life is still beautiful."

M.-S.C.C.

1. *Vogue Paris*, March 1939, 48.
2. *Harper's Bazaar*, June 2, 1937, 64.
3. Musée des Arts Décoratifs, Paris, inv. UF D 73-21-2238.
4. Philadelphia Museum of Art, Philadelphia, inv. 1969-232-27 a,b.

Design drawing, evening dress, summer 1939 collection. Musée des Arts Décoratifs, Paris, gift of Elsa Schiaparelli, Ufac, 1973, inv. UF-D-73-21-2238.

François Kollar, *Three Young Women in Evening Dresses with Bustles*, photograph, June 29, 1939.

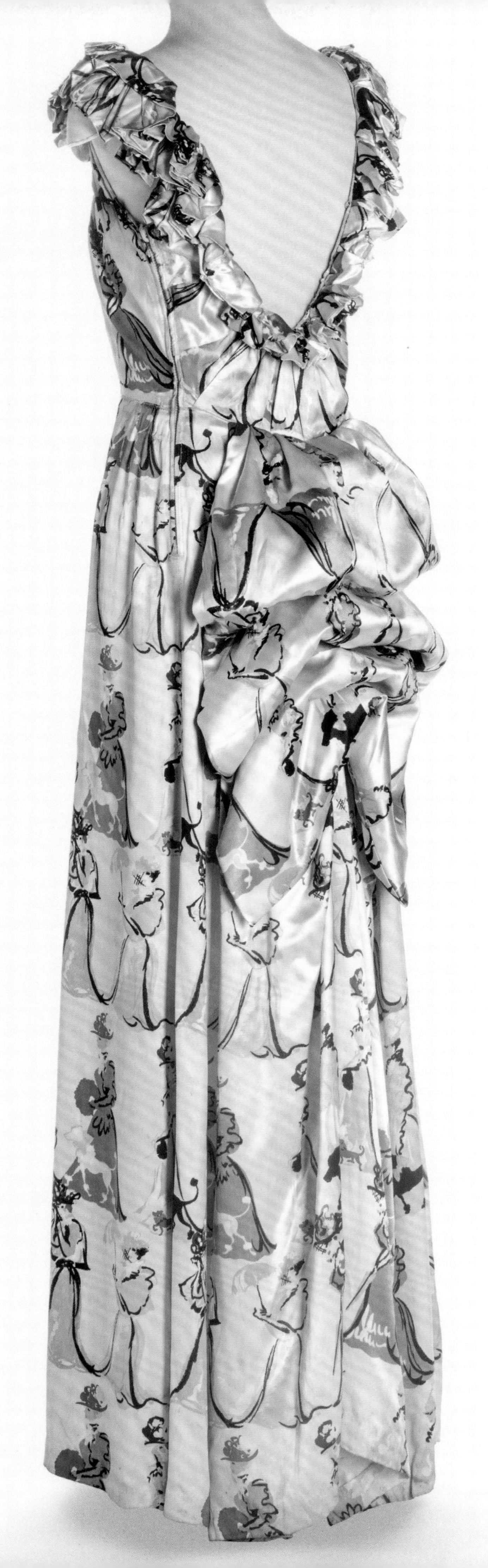

EVENING ENSEMBLE
Fall 1939

Organza, filé, and bead embroidery by Lesage, painted metal buttons
Gift of Patricia López-Willshaw, Ufac, 1966
Inv. UF 66-38-8 A and UF 66-38-5

By the late 1930s, each of the four annual collections presented by Elsa Schiaparelli was built around a strong, easily recognizable theme. This innovative idea was also a pretext for staging the fashion shows that "had a first-night aura of excitement to them at her openings," writes Bettina Ballard, the *Vogue* fashion editor, in her memoirs.[1] Thus, each collection was a much-anticipated artistic and society event that offered its share of stylistic innovations and impertinence.

This fall collection, whose theme was music, included approximately eighty items for day, leisure, and evening. The music theme was materialized in certain leitmotifs the designer integrated, for example, in the ornamentation: musical instrument embroidered on skirts, musical score prints for shirts, or scarves and many other variations; a real melody was even present thanks to a clever, miniature music box inserted inside a belt buckle.

The season's line defined a "sylph-like silhouette whose line was uninterrupted from neck to knee,"[2] in the example of this evening outfit comprising a long, fitted bodice in mauve organdy with embroidered flowers and foliage. The musical theme is found in the silver, tambourin-shaped jeweled buttons, probably made by Jean Schlumberger; the bodice is worn over a long dress in ivory albene with a low-cut back, and the skirt has stepped panels to suggest volume at the hips. This historical line, "the 1880s silhouette," according to *Femina* magazine,[3] illustrated Schiaparelli's continued interest in late nineteenth-century fashions that had already inspired the evening dresses in her previous collection. A series of drawings and fashion engravings from the same era[4] help us understand her sources of inspiration and creative process, she used details like the shape of a bodice or the curve of a silhouette.

This ensemble, acquired by one of her important clients and close friend, the South American Patricia López-Willshaw, had a few variations in the collection: a similar outfit with a black bodice embroidered with small bells and gold was selected by Schiaparelli for Marcel L'Herbier's dreamy short film *La Mode rêvée* that featured creations from the top couture houses of Paris and was shown at the 1939 New York World's Fair.

M.-P.R.

1. Bettina Ballard, *In My Fashion* (London: Secker & Warburg, 1960), 70.
2. Press release, April 1939, Maison Schiaparelli.
3. *Femina*, June 1939, 27.
4. The designer gave these engravings and drawings to Ufac in 1973. They are now in the Musée des Arts Décoratifs.

Vogue, July 1 1939, p. 30.
Illustration by Éric.

EVENING OUTFIT
Fall 1939

Silk satin embroidered with lamellae and metallic threads, appliqué celluloid sequins, metal buttons
Gift of Elsa Schiaparelli, Ufac, 1973
Inv. UF 73-21-27 AB

This silk satin ensemble, a jacket decorated on the bust with embroidered trompe l'oeil harps and wide pants with a zipper, is one of the rare evening pant suits designed by Elsa Schiaparelli that the museum has acquired. Ensembles like this appeared beginning with her first collections in 1928 and were exclusively destined for sports or leisure activities at the seashore.

The pajama or beach suit, a garment with fluid, comfortable pants, often in silk, was an essential, fashionable summer outfit as the new decade began. During the same period, Schiaparelli also proposed lounging pajamas for evening in her collections. This particularly sophisticated hostess outfit, similar to a negligee, met the period's demands for chic, relaxed outfits. This type of ensemble could take many forms: for her winter 1936–37 collection, Schiaparelli designed a hybrid evening dress that revealed fluid pants in front so the entire look resembled an oriental outfit. Other ensembles featured pants that were so wide, noted *Vogue*, that they almost looked like a skirt.[1] Schiaparelli also decorated the bodices or jackets of her pajamas with rich embroidery. These outfits were often purchased by the most prominent, elegant women of the era, such as Daisy Fellowes, one of her greatest clients.[2]

This short-sleeved model, destined for summer evenings, was part of the fall 1939 Music collection, a period during which Schiaparelli proposed "stay at home" pant suits whose dressier, slightly stricter style borrowed elements from the masculine wardrobe. There was a progressive appearance[3] of structured tweed suit jackets paired with slightly narrower pants with marked front pleats such as a violet cloque silk model chosen by Marlene Dietrich in 1937. Schiaparelli thus created an "*entre-deux*"[4] that was bit more formal than pajamas since their use began to wane by the late 1930s. These outfits were perhaps inspired by the androgynous style of her friend and loyal client, the star of *The Blue Angel*, who ordered a few of these outfits from her. Some of these pieces are now in the Deutsche Kinemathek collection in Berlin.

M.-P.R.

1. *Vogue*, June 1, 1931, 65.
2. *Vogue*, August 15, 1935, 34.
3. Spring 1937, summer 1938, and winter 1938–39 collections.
4. Catherine Join-Diéterle, "Marlene à l'écran, à la ville, une garde-robe feminine," in *Marlene Dietrich, création d'un mythe*, exh. cat. (Paris: Paris Musées, 2003), 82.

Unknown photographer, *Elsa Schiaparelli and her daughter Gogo on holidays in Monte Carlo*, photograph, 1938

EVENING ENSEMBLE
Fall 1939

Ducharne silk scarf print, painted metallic buttons by Jean Schlumberger
Gift of Patricia López-Willshaw, Ufac, 1966
Inv. UF 66-38-2 ABCD

Presented in April 1939, the Music collection for the fall of the same year also featured summer outfits, including this sophisticated dinner ensemble. It was part of the wardrobe of Patricia López-Willshaw, one of Maison Schiaparelli's important clients who collected some of the most iconic pieces of the designer's work.

Comprising an unusual sleeveless bolero and a long dress with low-cut back, this outfit evokes the collection's dominant line of a slim, elongated silhouette; it was designed in a silk scarf print from Ducharne and its pattern of small alternating garnet, white, and Nattier blue checks was a motif used for the Commedia dell'arte collection the previous spring. Its vaguely historical silhouette is livened up at the center front by the musical leitmotif, a series of six small, enameled metal buttons, each in the shape of a drum.

In contrast with other couture designers of her era, Schiaparelli's buttons are figurative, fantastic, extremely unusual and often worked in symbiosis with the collection theme (see p. 201). "In spite of the zippers, King Button still reigned without fear at Schiap's. The most incredible things were used, animals and feathers, caricatures . . . but not one looked like what a button was supposed to look like."[1] For the Music collection, a variety of small instruments passed through buttonholes such as the enameled ceramic pianos[2] made by Jean Clement. The small drums are the work of Jean Schlumberger, who also designed a large number of costume jewelry pieces for Schiaparelli between 1937 and 1939, a true repertory of colorful, reworked, impertinent shapes that included hand clips, feather combs, a necklace made of small swings with angels dangling on them, shell buttons, etc. Some even appeared in a portrait that Leonor Fini painted of Schiaparelli in 1939.[3]

M.-P.R.

1. Elsa Schiaparelli, *Shocking Life* (London: J.M. Dent & Sons, 195), 98.
2. Musée des Arts Décoratifs, Paris, inv. 2012.48.2342.
3. Musée des Arts Décoratifs, Paris, inv. 2009.112.3.

Harper's Bazaar, July 1939, p. 48. Photograph by George Hoyningen-Huene.

Design drawing, evening ensemble, fall 1939 collection. Musée des Arts Décoratifs, Paris, gift of Elsa Schiaparelli, Ufac, 1973, inv. UF-D-73-21-2357.

EVENING DRESS
Winter 1939–40

Ducharne faconne silk velvet on a satin ground
Gift of Elsa Schiaparelli, Ufac, 1973
Inv. UF 73-21-5

This evening dress was shown to the public on August 3, 1939, one month before France entered the war. Because of her fame, the designer launched her new collection for the following winter as international relationships were deteriorating yet paradoxically, the climate in Paris was quite festive: "Paris has suddenly been having a fit of prosperity, gaiety, and hospitality."[1]

This collection was not based on a specific theme but rather proposed a reflection on a silhouette Elsa Schiaparelli called the Cigarette Silhouette. In the press release written by her communications director, the American Hortense MacDonald, the "typical model"[2] of the collection was day suit no. 443[3] in brown wool with a long, broad-shouldered jacket and a skirt that was fitted on the hips, combined with a dress developed in different variations whose skirt was constructed like a flounced apron raised up on the sides. This svelte silhouette, which hugged the body's curves, was a continuation of the slender cuts that had been proposed the previous season. Generally, the Cigarette Silhouette collection dresses followed this guiding principle, seen in this evening model with a low-cut bodice, marked waist, and long skirt structured by loose draping along the hips. Schiaparelli also excelled in inventing unique volumes and folds that she workd on live models, like a sculptor, to create new pieces; the choice of fabric in this creative process was crucial and she worked closely with textile manufacturers. This dress was cut in a luxurious silk velvet with satin ground from Maison Ducharne in Lyon, run at the time by François Ducharne: "It was a pleasure to work with Madame Schiaparelli who loved spun silks and even daring ones. I collaborated with her by submitting original sketches, which she would adopt and then choose the colors herself."[4]

M.-P.R.

1. Janet Flanner, *Paris Was Yesterday* (New York: Harcourt Brace Jovanovich, 1972), 220.

2. Press releases, August 1939, Maison Schiaparelli.

3. Musée des Arts Décoratifs, Paris, inv. UF D 73-21-2465.

4. François Ducharne, "En ce temps-là, la soie. Souvenirs," *Les Folles Années de la soie* (Lyon: Musée Historique des Tissus, 1975), 33.

Design drawing, evening dress, winter 1939–40 collection. Musée des Arts Décoratifs, Paris, gift of Elsa Schiaparelli, Ufac, 1973, inv. UF-D-73-21-2500.

EVENING COAT
Winter 1939–40

Faconne silk velvet with satin ground, gold-plated buttons
Gift of Elsa Schiaparelli, Ufac, 1973
Inv. UF 73-21-22

This long evening coat in faconne velvet on a satin ground features a pattern of red dots against a black ground. The jacket part of the coat is closed by eleven gold-plated red buttons. The coat ends in a train that is highlighted in the collection drawing.

The winter 1939–40 collection was presented to clients and the press in the Place Vendôme couture salon on August 3, 1939. *Vogue*'s Paris correspondent Bettina Ballard evoked the unusual mood that reigned at Schiaparelli: "Her gold-and-white salon on the Place Vendôme had a first-night aura of excitement to them at her openings. The best seats were reserved for her smartest customers: Millicent Rogers, the Honourable Mrs. Regina Fellowes, Contessa Gab de Robilant, Contessa Cora Caetani, the Marquise de Polignac, and such notable devotees. The stairs would be filled with artists, writers, musicians, decorators—all the creative people around Paris. The small salon would contain the crowded uncomfortable press."[1] The exceptional quality of the collection's fabrics were noted in the program written by the brilliant press attaché Hortense MacDonald, who alluded to the international events on the eve of war: "The fabrics are lavish. Lots of velvet. . . . We thank France's manufacturers for this renaissance of sumptuous fabrics. In this stormy year, we must applaud them."[2]

With its rich fabric, slim corseted waist, and curved line accentuating the train, this evening coat stands out from the rest of the collection. It is clear, in looking at the nineteenth-century fashion illustrations from *Le Journal des demoiselles* that Elsa Schiaparelli gave to Ufac, that the coat's line was inspired by the fin de siècle tastes of the 1880s and 1890s.

In summer 1939, the designer closed the London boutique she had opened five years earlier. She admitted in her memoirs that the insecure feeling omnipresent in Europe at the time caused her to make this decision.[3]

On September 3, exactly one month after the collection was presented, Great Britain and then France declared war on Germany. All the Paris couture houses' activities, which had slowed down as men mobilized for war, continued in a scaled-down manner.

M.-S.C.C.

1. Bettina Ballard, *In My Fashion* (London: Secker & Warburg, 1960), 70.

2. Maison Schiaparelli.

3. Elsa Schiaparelli, *Shocking Life* (London: J. M. Dent & Sons, 1954), 108.

Design drawing, evening coat, winter 1939–40 collection. Musée des Arts Décoratifs, Paris, gift of Elsa Schiaparelli, Ufac, 1973, inv. UF D 73-21-2531.

Journal des demoiselles, fashion engraving, c. 1885. Musée des Arts Décoratifs, Paris, gift of Elsa Schiaparelli, Ufac, 1973.

DAY COAT
Spring 1940

Wool twill, leather, and metal buttons
Gift of Patricia López-Willshaw, Ufac, 1966
Inv. UF 66-38-7

This coat, one of Elsa Schiaparelli's iconic creations, was made during the difficult context at the beginning of World War II. Despite the conflict, Parisian fashion houses, under the leadership of Lucien Lelong, head of the Chambre Syndicale de la Couture, remained active. *Vogue Paris* summed up the situation by underlining how much they had been able to "transform the brilliant fashions they proposed this fall into creations whose sober elegance were tactfully in line with the moment's requirements."[1] This was also the case of Elsa Schiaparelli who reimagined her October collection for the following spring despite reduced capital and significant drop in her staff from 600 to 150 people. Because of this, for spring 1940 she imagined a "small war collection"[2] of thirty models, mostly fairly sober day outfits with no accessories. According to the designer, "We built up a collection in three weeks hoping for some response. This was the 'Cash and Carry' collection."[3]

The military uniform's influence on the designs presented, lauded for their practical elegance, was clear, especially in the slightly martial look of certain coats and jackets, as well as in the choice of colors like "Legion red," "airplane gray," and "Maginot line blue," similar to the "Royal Air Force blue" coat launched at the same time by Captain Molyneux.[4] Beyond this stylistic influence, widespread in the Paris couture shows, the collection was characterized by inventiveness like an evening dress that could be transformed into a day dress; or an unusual woolen jumpsuit with a long front zipper that had four huge pockets,[5] an ideal outfit for elegantly taking refuge in an underground shelter during a bomb alert.

The enormous, slightly detached pockets were the collection's leitmotif. We see them placed on the side of this day coat, which used to belong to Patricia López-Willshaw. These buttoned and zipped "pouch pockets" stood in for bags, which were not included in the collection, so a woman could carry her important papers and objects. This military-look coat was cut in sturdy wool, qualified as a "waterproof tweed" by *L'Officiel*,[6] a new textile featured by the house that season. The garment's giant buttons with the famous S logo enlivened the blue fabric. Halfway between a utilitarian piece of clothing and a couture creation, this coat also echoed the coat and suit drawer pockets that the designer had produced in collaboration with Salvador Dalí in 1936 (see p. 45).

M.-P.R.

1. *Paris-couture-années trente*, ed. Guillaume Garnier (Paris: musée de la Mode et du Costume, 1987), 240.
2. Press release, October 1939, Maison Schiaparelli.
3. Elsa Schiaparelli, *Shocking Life* (London: J. M. Dent & Sons, 1954), 113–14.
4. Edward Molyneux.
5. The jumpsuit is now in the Musée du Château Borély – Musée des Arts Décoratifs, de la Faïence et de la Mode, Marseille, inv. 995.4.1.
6. *L'Officiel de la couture et de la mode*, October–November 1939, 18.

Design drawing, evening jacket, spring 1940 collection. Musée des Arts Décoratifs, Paris, gift of Elsa Schiaparelli, Ufac, 1973, inv. UF-D-73-21-2383.

Vogue, 15 December 1939, p. 40. Photograph by Agneta Fischer.

EVENING JACKET
Spring 1947

Pekin silk, filé, lamella, and sequin embroidery and appliqués
Gift of Elsa Schiaparelli, Ufac, 1973
Inv. UF 73-21-60

This spectacular evening jacket, originally paired with a long, low-cut blue dress, was presented at the beginning of November 1946 during the mid-season show for the following spring. For the outfits and evening dresses, Schiaparelli once again accented a vaguely historical silhouette whose line she had already reinterpreted as of 1939. Since she returned to Paris in July 1945 and with her first collection being shown in September, the designer took up the inspirations that had guided her in the 1930s: a slender silhouette with longer proportions, a taste for strong ornamentation, and a look to fashions from the past, such as her Directoire collection for winter 1945–46.

These tendencies were echoed for fall 1946, especially in the pouf effects at the bottom of some jackets, skirts, and evening dresses: "Schiaparelli, more bustle style!" was *Women's Wear Daily* headline.[1] The designer also proposed variations on her highly embroidered prewar evening jacket models such as this luxurious pekin silk jacket manufactured by the Jacotte workshop with a fitted line that sat on the hips and rounded shoulders accentuated by clever pleating. Here, Schiaparelli reminds us of the masterful cutting technique incarnated by Monsieur René, considered by many to be the best tailor in Paris.

This femininity with its "hard, highly individual chic"[2] and almost theatrical effect also appeared in a dinner outfit, a major piece in the collection whose jacket, now in the Philadelphia Museum of Art,[3] is in black crepe decorated with shocking pink edges embroidered in scrolls of jet beads that extend into a bustle. The garment recalls the splendor and flair of sixteenth-century France.[4] At the same time, Schiaparelli returned to her fascination for the court of Louis XIV by launching a new perfume, Le Roy Soleil, whose luxurious Baccarat crystal bottle, sold in a limited edition of 2,000 pieces, was designed by Salvador Dalí.

M.-P.R.

1. "Schiaparelli, more bustle style!" *Women's Wear Daily*, November 6, 1946, 3.

2. Bettina Ballard, *In My Fashion* (London: Secker & Warburg, 1960), 62.

3. Philadelphia Museum of Art, inv. 1969-232-24.

4. Dilys E. Blum, *Shocking! The Art and Fashion of Elsa Schiaparelli*, exh. cat. (Philadelphia: Philadelphia Museum of Art, 2003), 264–67.

Design drawing, evening jacket, spring 1947 collection. Musée des Arts Décoratifs, Paris, gift of Elsa Schiaparelli, Ufac, 1973, inv. UF-D-73-21-3836.

SKIRT
Winter 1948–49

Ducharne pekin taffeta, silk crepe
Gift of Elsa Schiaparelli, Ufac, 1973
Inv. UF 73-21-2

This striking skirt was presented as part of the winter 1947–48 collection on August 4, 1947. Its line was inspired[1] by the daring bottle for Schiaparelli's perfume Zut, which shows the legs of a woman whose skirt has fallen to her feet, revealing her undergarments.

This collection, introduced six months after Christian Dior's Corolle line, was characterized by innovations in the treatment of certain skirts: "The wool ones are straight and slim the silhouette, the cocktail skirts look like a cone hooped at the bottom, varying from very narrow to very wide. . . . Shell-like shapes sometimes spiral over the front or back,"[2] explains the press release. For the first time, the designer introduced stays, sewn into the hems, to give them fullness or the desired shape as seen in this evening skirt. Cut in a pekin taffeta from Ducharne, the spectacular volume is supported by stays that spiral up the back and form an apron in front. With this sculptural piece, Schiaparelli once again revived the pouf or bustle, whose artistic possibilities she had been exploring since the late 1930s. But unlike the late nineteenth-century bustle, where the mechanism was hidden inside the garment, here the structure that forms the volume is fully visible and creates a spectacular effect for this skirt that, as seen in the sketch, was worn with a simple black silk jersey fitted bodice.

The designer also highlights a tartan pattern, which was also popular in fin de siècle women's fashions and that she regularly used for day or leisure outfits and coats. Here, she gives it an unexpected vividness by using it for evening as she did a few years before with a plaid dress from the summer 1939 collection.[3]

M.-P.R.

1. Press release, August 1947, Maison Schiaparelli.
2. Ibid.
3. Palais Galliera, Paris, inv. Gal 1992-3 xAB.

Design drawing, skirt, winter 1948–49 collection. Musée des Arts Décoratifs, Paris, gift of Elsa Schiaparelli, Ufac, 1973, inv. UF-D-73-21-5132.

Unknown photographer, *Ball Hosted by Étienne de Beaumont*, photograph, 1950.

EVENING ENSEMBLE
Fall 1949

Shot taffeta
Gift of Elsa Schiaparelli, Ufac, 1973
Inv. UF 73-21-32

This skirt and bodice evening ensemble in shot taffeta is one of two examples from Schiaparelli's fall 1949 collection—presented in May of the same year—now in the Musée des Arts Décoratifs. After the Hurricane line she designed for summer with full silhouettes that were projected to the back or front as if lifted by gusts of wind (recalling her spring 1934 Aerodynamic collection), Schiaparelli designed a collection whose theme was the point.[1] The leitmotif was developed in oversized, curved, pointed collars, irregularly cut asymmetric décolletés and bustiers on dresses or bathing suits with matching helmet hats. The skirts, as in this outfit, were sometimes cut in layered, pointed petals whose fullness, molded by stays, was draped over a sheath skirt. Like most of the collection's pieces, this outfit had no ornaments, thus accenting a very defined waist emphasized by the skirt volume and natural shoulder line.

This outfit probably belonged to Elsa Schiaparelli herself. Although her gift to Ufac included mainly pieces or prototypes from her archives and collections, we also note the presence of garments from her own wardrobe. A famous photo of the designer with Salvador Dalí, taken by Cecil Beaton in 1950 during a soirée in Neuilly at the home of their mutual friends Arturo and Patricia López-Willshaw, shows her dressed in this ensemble. It is interesting to note that for the event, she accented her outfit with a crown of ivy that was originally worn as a necklace with an evening outfit from her Pagan collection. She also pinned to her bodice her famous brooch depicting the Great Bear constellation that, according to her uncle, the famous astronomer Giovanni Schiaparelli, could be seen in the beauty spots on her left cheek.

M.-P.R.

1. *Women's Wear Daily*, May 5, 1949, 5.

Design drawing, evening ensemble, autumn 1949 collection. Musée des Arts Décoratifs, Paris, gift of Elsa Schiaparelli, Ufac, 1973, inv. UF-D-73-21-4375.

Unknown photographer, *Elsa Schiaparelli and Salvador Dalí at the López Residence*, photograph, 1949.

EVENING JACKET Spring 1950

Silk velvet with appliqué braids and sequin embroidery by Lesage
Gift of Elsa Schiaparelli, Ufac, 1973
Inv. UF 73-21-37

This red silk velvet jacket embroidered by Lesage was part of the spring 1950 collection shown in the couture house's Place Vendôme salons on November 26, 1949. The collection press release defined a geometric line that focused on volume and dynamic movement. Shown in profile in the sketch,[1] the jacket, worn over a dress, is made up of square panels similar to a house of cards. The graded, colored lines of plastic sequins attached to a black braid that emphasize the jacket contours illuminated the jacket when it moved.

The Metropolitan Museum of Art in New York also has a model of this jacket, which is attributed to Hubert de Givenchy.[2] Hired by Elsa Schiaparelli in 1947 to design the Place Vendôme's boutique collections, the young Hubert de Givenchy rounded off his knowledge of the profession and developed the foundation for his future style. He also made advantageous contacts. He left Schiaparelli in 1951 and opened Givenchy the following year. He remembers the fashion designer's working methods: "I sometimes proposed a group of sketches and she choose a few. She then asked her *premier d'atelier* to make some of the styles under her supervision. They didn't always correspond to what I had intended."[3]

In 1950 American *Vogue* praised Madame Schiaparelli, noting that she was still an influential fashion designer and eminent personality in Paris society. The article continued by adding that her vivacity, intuition, and originality offered a new idea each season whether it was a color, a silhouette, or a trend[4]. Schiaparelli was still the best ambassador for her label with the American fashion press, such as *Vogue*, and was also featured in mask-market magazines, appearing on the cover of *Newsweek*[5].

M.-S.C.C.

1. Musée des Arts Décoratifs, Paris, inv. UF D 73-21-4699 (see p. 180).

2. Metropolitan Museum of Art, New York, inv. 1973.52a-c.

3. "Schiaparelli et Christian Bérard par Hubert de Givenchy," in *Schiaparelli et les artistes* (Paris: Rizzoli, 2017), 120.

4. *Vogue*, March 1, 1950, 7.

5. *Newsweek*, September 26, 1949, front cover title: "Schiaparelli the Shocker."

Design drawing, jacket and evening dress, spring 1950 collection. Musée des Arts Décoratifs, Paris, gift of Elsa Schiaparelli, Ufac, 1973, inv. UF D 73-21-4699.

Unknown photographer, *Woman Wearing a Schiaparelli Evening Jacket*, photograph, November 26, 1949.

EVENING DRESS
Winter 1950–51

Silk satin, silk velvet, embroidery by Lesage of metallic-thread braid, cordonnet, bead, and rhinestone appliqués
Gift of Elsa Schiaparelli, Ufac, 1973
Inv. UF 73-21-30

This evening dress with its particularly luxurious decoration came from the winter 1950–51 Front Line collection presented on August 1, 1950. The season's silhouette was summed up in the press release: "Madame Schiaparelli . . . likes a perfect waist at its natural place, a bust, hips, and rounded shoulders, curved, slim legs and an absolutely flat tummy."[1] The original feature of this collection, echoing its name, was the use of a small oval board of wood or plastic inserted in a stomach-level pocket in some models so the abdomen would be perfectly flat. This artifice, disapproved of by American retailers[2] since it was not adaptable to their clientele, emphasized the slender line and tight waist that characterized suits of the era such as those worn by Wallis, Duchess of Windsor who was immortalized by Irving Penn in *Vogue* wearing suit no. 418.[3]

This princess-line evening dress,[4] an unusual model in the collection, illustrates a that season's trend for short hemlines; the cone-shaped skirt is structured at the bottom by a stay inside the hem in the spirit of the "lampshade" tunics Paul Poiret made fashionable in 1911. Cut in a satin richly embroidered with beads and spun gold threads that formed botehs (paisley motifs), it reminds us of the designer's interest in the Orient, which she began to reinterpret in the mid-1930s with her sari dresses (summer 1935) and bodices with embroidered necklines evoking Persian calligraphy (winter 1936–37).

Schiaparelli had fun with the Oriental drama of this dress and wore it to a costume ball of tableaux vivants, also known as the "ball at the eighteenth-century French court" given by Jacques Fath at the Château de Corbeville in June 1952. For the event, she accessorized it with a long slip and majestic feathered turban similar to the one she wore to the Oriental Ball organized by the Honorable Reginald Fellowes in the summer of 1935.

M.-P.R.

1. Press release, August 1950, Maison Schiaparelli.

2. *Women's Wear Daily*, August 10, 1950, 10.

3. *Vogue*, March 1, 1951, 165. Sketch now in the Musée des Arts Décoratifs, inv. UF d 73- 21-4829.

4. Dress with no waist seam.

Design drawing, evening dress, winter 1950–51 collection. Musée des Arts Décoratifs, Paris, gift of Elsa Schiaparelli, Ufac, 1973, inv. UF-D-73-21-4906.

Unknown photographer, *Elsa Schiaparelli at the Bal des Tableaux Vivants*, photograph, june 1951.

EVENING JACKET
Spring 1951

Silk satin, mink fur appliqués, embroidered with tinsel, rhinestones, tubes, beads, and chenille by Lesage
Gift of Elsa Schiaparelli, Ufac, 1973
Inv. UF 73-21-54

This piece from the spring 1951 collection, presented in the Schiaparelli couture salons on November 14, 1950, is spectacular thanks to the exceptional quality of its Lesage embroidery and its full, oversized skirt, which evokes the New Look promoted by Christian Dior. After returning from the United States in 1947, Hubert de Givenchy was hired by Elsa Schiaparelli at the age of twenty as creative director of her boutique on the Place Vendôme. He remained there four years before opening his own couture house. In 1950 the journalist Susan Train, Paris correspondent for American *Vogue*, mentioned the elegant clients' fondness for the Schiaparelli boutique, an address where everyone could find unique accessories.[1] The boutique's success helped maintain the label's renown. Asked many times by his friend Christian Dior to work for him, Givenchy was retained by Schiaparelli, who continued to promise him more responsibilities for the boutique collection her clients adored. On the other hand, it seemed that Schiaparelli did not want him to help design the couture line with a few exceptions,[2] such as this evening jacket.

In 1951 Maison Schiaparelli had not recaptured its pre-war luster, although clients such as Patricia López-Willshaw and the Duchess of Windsor remained loyal. Schiaparelli once again called on the figurative embroidery of Maison Lesage for this model featuring botanical decoration of chestnut motifs in rhinestones and mink, chenille leaves, and tinsel highlighted by beading. The embroidery for this model was produced by François Lesage, who had taken over his father Albert's embroidery company in 1949. He remembers his collaboration with "Schiap" and analyzes the different embroidery concepts at Balmain, Fath, and Dior in the early 1950s: "Our work for them, less narrative and more simply ornamental with a base of arabesques and rinceaux, was very different from what we did for Schiaparelli."[3] At Schiaparelli's, he remembered meeting Hubert de Givenchy, who was considered "something of an heir apparent" to the couturiere.[4] Dominique Sirop, a designer and fashion historian, attributed this evening jacket to Hubert de Givenchy in 2015 because of a drawing found in the Schiaparelli archives: the sketch of the redingote-shaped jacket's back with a very long point is annotated and signed "Hubert de Givenchy."[5]

M.-S.C.C.

1. Susan Train, "Notes sur une carrière observée," *Givenchy, 40 ans de création,* exh. cat. (Paris: Paris-Musées, 1991).
2. Like the jacket in the Metropolitan Museum of Art, inv. 1971.52a-c.
3. "Broder pour "Schiap", conversation avec François Lesage," *Hommage à Schiaparelli* (Paris: Musée de la Mode et du Costume, 1984).
4. Ibid.
5. Maison Schiaparelli.

Hubert de Givenchy, drawing of the Schiaparelli spring 1951 collection evening ensemble, drawn in 2014. Maison Schiaparelli, Paris.

Design drawing, jacket and evening dress, spring 1951 collection. Musée des Arts Décoratifs, Paris, gift of Elsa Schiaparelli, Ufac, 1973, inv. UF-D-73-21-4936.

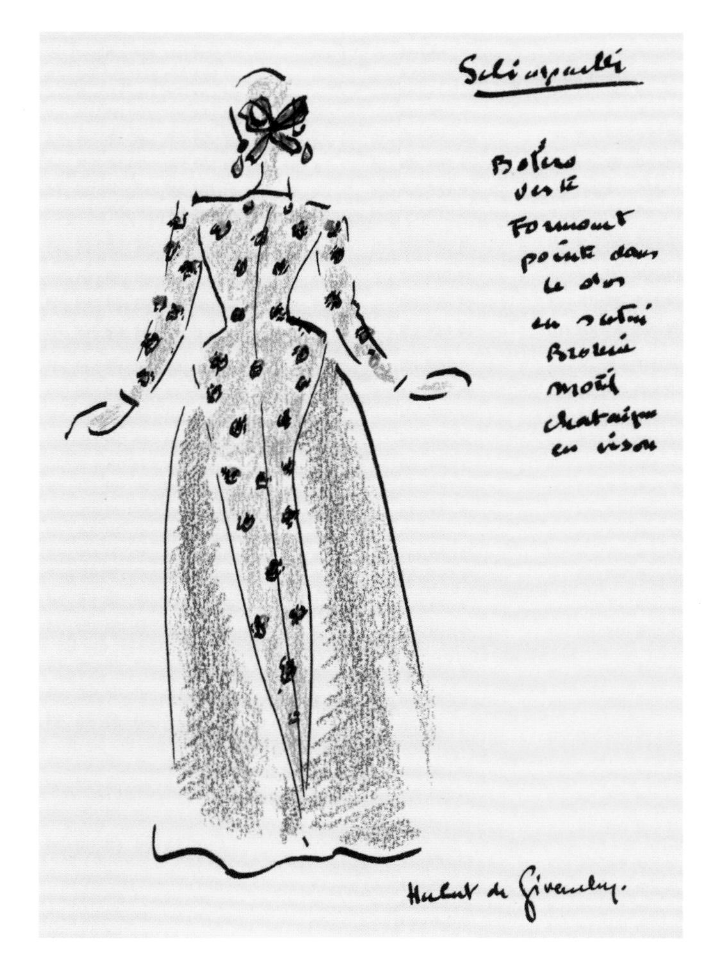

PAIR OF LONG GLOVES
Winter 1951–52

Silk velvet
Gift of Elsa Schiaparelli, Ufac, 1973
UF 73-21-40 AB

This pair of emerald silk velvet gloves was presented on July 29, 1951 during the show for the winter 1951–52 collection. Worn with a generous gray-black coat as seen in the sketch[1] now in the Musée des Arts Décoratifs, the gloves covered the arms with long puffy sleeves.

Gloves, an obligatory fashion accessory at the time, were important elements of the poetic surrealism that occupied a special place in Elsa Schiaparelli's work, especially during the 1930s. By showing what they hid and hiding what they showed,[2] they incarnated a visual, sometimes fantastic ambiguity that was so important to the designer.

In the early 1950s, Schiaparelli was also inspired by the formal extravagance of the Baroque period, which she reinterprets here in a theatrical, unbalanced movement. The only design of its type in the collection yet representative of a trend at the time, they were referred to as "balloon gloves in a peaceful color" in the press release.[3] The text also announced the season's theme, SHAPE, named after the Supreme Headquarters Allied Powers Europe that had been directed by General Eisenhower since April 2, 1951.[4] This title is not only a reference to current events but also a pretext to define a new line whose shape was poetically inspired by the ebb and flow of waves on the beach. The designer also played with nautical references by giving evocative names like "black sea" or "ocean green" to her new colors and, unusually for her, to garments themselves such as the Oursin (sea urchin) dress.[5] She also brought the theme to life by draping or puffing up fabrics in the front or back like the evening dress with a bustle that she gave to the Metropolitan Museum of New York in 1951.[6]

M.-P.R.

1. Musée des Arts Décoratifs, Paris, inv. UF d 73-21-5372 (see p. 192).

2. Bernard Vouilloux, "Mains et merveilles. Petit manuel du surréalisme," *Modernités 16* "Enchantements. Mélanges offerts à Yves Vadé" (Pessac: Presses universitaires de Bordeaux, 2002), 161.

3. Press release, August 1951, Maison Schiaparelli.

4. *Women's Wear Daily*, July 30, 1951, 3.

5. Press release, August 1951, Maison Schiaparelli.

6. Metropolitan Museum of Art, New York, inv. C.I.51.110.1.

Vogue Paris, November 1951, p. 21. Photograph by Henry Clarke.

Design drawing, long gloves, winter 1951–52 collection. Musée des Arts Décoratifs, Paris, gift of Elsa Schiaparelli, Ufac, 1973, inv. UF-D-73-21-5372.

EVENING DRESS
Winter 1952–53

Silk satin, taffeta
Gift of Elsa Schiaparelli, Ufac, 1973
Inv. UF 73-21-31

This evening dress is from the winter 1952–53 collection whose theme was the cicada. Returning to her taste for metamorphosis, Schiaparelli again focused on one of the tiny insects she had used to decorate her jackets, accessories, and jewelry for the fall 1938 Pagan collection. The inspiration of the Jean de la Fontaine character, "who despite the fable, continues to sing this winter,"[1] is conveyed through peplums or prominent, double, protruding drapings that imitate the insect's wings when folded on its back as well as forward-pointing oversized collars that break the silhouette's line, and embroidery and buttons in the shape of cicadas. Other models featured special volumes, especially at the hips, like this sheath dress that reused the idea of an upside-down heart décolleté, already a sensation in the summer 1952 collection. As if enveloped in taffeta, this two-color model has one oversized puffed sleeve whose opulent draping is pushed up on a hand sheathed in a blue satin glove. The asymmetrical dress reflects a baroque mood and once again recalls the designer's taste and mastery for the volumes she modeled: "A sculptor? The dream of being a Pygmalion could have been irresistible. Sculpture seems to me to be one of the arts nearest to creation. The feeling of moulding between one's fingers a shape mirrored in one's mind is one of intense magnetism and divine sensuality."[2]

A savvy communicator, Schiaparelli orchestrated the launch of her collection by placing a giant grasshopper dressed in the latest Paris fashions[3] in a window of her boutique before the fashion show; this was organized in an unusual location for the period, the courtyard of her own town house on the Rue de Berri, decorated for the event "like a Cocteau play."[4] Held at 10:30 p.m. on August 1, 1952, for a select group of clients including the American actress and dancer Ginger Rogers and the "cream of international buyers,"[5] the show was followed by a party featuring a Brazilian orchestra that lasted into the wee hours.

M.-P.R.

1. Press release, August 1952, Maison Schiaparelli.
2. Elsa Schiaparelli, *Shocking Life* (London: J. M. Dent & Sons, 1954), 225–26.
3. *Women's Wear Daily*, August 1, 1952, 3.
4. *L'Intransigeant*, August 2, 1952, 6F.
5. Ibid.

Design drawing, evening dress, winter 1952–53 collection. Musée des Arts Décoratifs, Paris, gift of Elsa Schiaparelli, Ufac, 1973, inv. UF-D-73-21-5744.

JEWELRY

Costume Jewelry and Accessories

The Schiaparelli look comprised a garment, accessories such as hats and gloves, and jewelry, which added a harmonious, ornamental touch to the whole—this was the work of artisans known as *paruriers*. They operated in the designer's shadow and did not sign their work. The theme of each collection was communicated to the *parurier*, who made suggestions for jewelry models. Elsa Schiaparelli surrounded herself with jewelry suppliers with strong personalities, capable of sharing her inventiveness and surprising her, as well as with artists who took other surprising creative paths. In her memoirs, she praises three of her collaborators who made costume jewelry that was a great success with her clients: the loyal Jean Clément, a craftsman considered a technical genius; Elsa Triolet, the woman of letters, for her novel aspirin necklaces; and the goldsmith François Hugo, the great-grandson of Victor Hugo, for his original buttons. Indeed, "King Button," as Elsa Schiaparelli put it, triumphed over the couture garment of which it was a part in the form of objects, sometimes outsized, made of innovative materials and in a blend of colors that made it different from a simple functional fastener. Taking the form of small sculptures, the buttons were genuine jewels that matched the outfit, adding an extra touch of magic and chic. Although Schiaparelli did not mention the jeweler Jean Schlumberger in her memoirs, he captured the designer's surrealist spirit with elegance and humor, creating a lively, colorful repertoire of costume jewelry to highlight the themes of the Pagan and Circus collections. Leonor Fini, who designed the Shocking perfume bottle, painted his portrait, depicting him as an Italian Renaissance goldsmith posing in front of his creations. The jewelry that Alberto Giacometti made for Schiaparelli between 1934 and 1939—after he abandoned surrealism—was an opportunity for him to experiment with new figurative and stylized forms on a very small scale. Close to Jean-Michel Frank, Giacometti was excluded from the surrealist group in 1934–35 by André Breton, who criticized him for producing decorative objects.

M.-S.C.C.

By Artists

1.

2.

3.

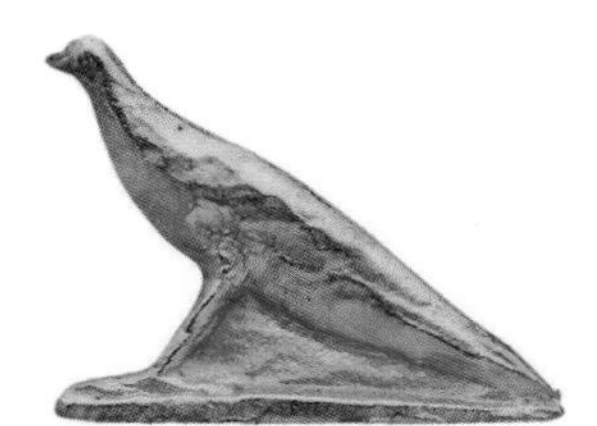

4.

5.

1. Alberto Giacometti
Angel of the Annunciation brooch, 1934–39
Gilt bronze, 9.5 × 5.1 cm
Maison Schiaparelli, Paris

2. Alberto Giacometti
Helix brooch, 1935–39
Silver, Diam. 4.6 cm
Private collection, Paris

3. Alberto Giacometti
Bird brooch, 1934–39
Gilt bronze, 5.5 × 4.5 cm
Private collection, Paris

4. Alberto Giacometti
Bird brooch, 1934–39
Gilt bronze, 3.5 × 3.5 cm
Private collection, Paris

5. Alberto Giacometti
Sphinx brooch, 1934–39
Gilt bronze, 6.5 × 5.1 cm
Private collection, Paris

6. Alberto Giacometti
Button, 1935–39
Gilt bronze, 4.5 × 4.3 cm
Private collection, Paris

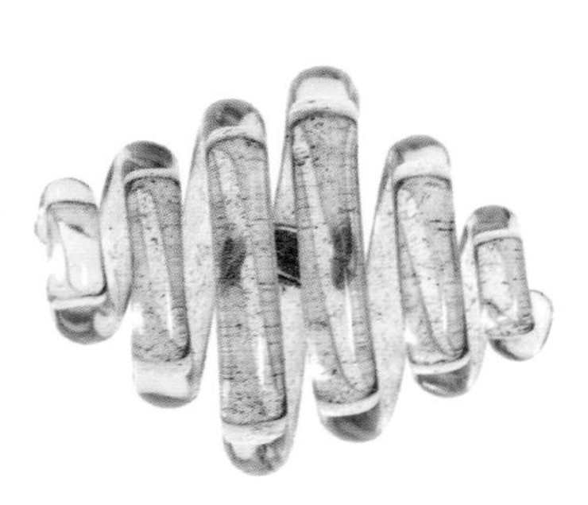

8.

9.

7. Alberto Giacometti
Button, 1937
Gilt bronze, Diam. 4.2 cm
Musée des Arts Décoratifs, Paris, formerly Loïc Allio collection Purchased thanks to the Fonds du Patrimoine et au Mécénat, 2012
Inv. 2012.48.1593

8. Elsa Triolet
Set of buttons, c. 1931
Colored glass shaped with a blowtorch,
2.7 × 3.8 cm
Musée des Arts Décoratifs, Paris, formerly Loïc Allio collection Purchased thanks to the Fonds du Patrimoine et au Mécénat, 2012
Inv. 2012.48.1635 to 1638

9. Meret Oppenheim
Fur bracelet, 1936
Metal and fur, Diam. 7 cm
Private collection, Paris

By *Paruriers*

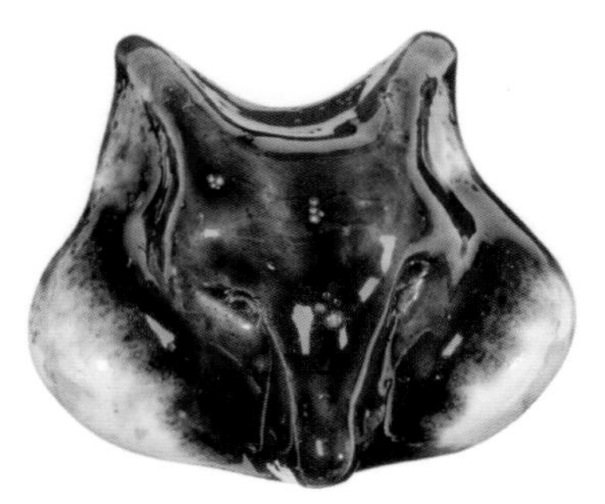

1.

2.

3.

4.

5.

6.

1. Jean Clément
Button, summer 1937
Enameled ceramic,
3.5 × 4 cm
Inv. 2012.48.2294.1

2. Jean Clément
Button, fall 1939
Enameled red clay,
2.1 × 1.9 cm
Inv. 2012.48.2342

3. Jean Clément
Button, 1930–49
Enameled ceramic,
Diam. 4.8 cm
Inv. 2012.48.2287

4. François Hugo
Button, 1940–49
Enameled ceramic,
Diam. 3.3 cm
Inv. 2012.48.1982

5. Jean Clément
Button, c. 1942
Enameled ceramic,
4.7 × 4.3 cm
Inv. 2012.48.2288

6. François Hugo
Button, 1940–49
Ink inscription on paper,
metal, and glass,
Diam. 3 cm
Inv. 2012.48.1901

7. Jean Clément
Button, 1930–49
Beetle and resin,
3.9 × 1.6 cm
Inv. 2012.48.2405

7.

8.

9.

10.

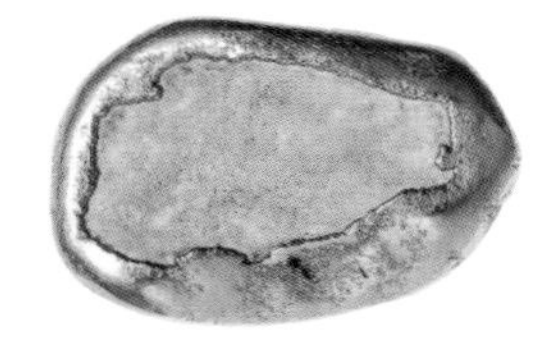

11.

12.

8. François Hugo
Button, 1940–49
Painted and enameled ceramic,
3.9 × 2.6 cm
Inv. 2012.48.1859

9. Jean Clément
Button, c. 1952
Resin, metal, and photograph under glass,
Diam. 1.3 cm
Inv. 2014.61.2

10. François Hugo
Button, 1940–49
Painted and enameled ceramic,
2.8 × 3.6 cm
Inv. 2012.48.1857

11. François Hugo
Button, 1941
Set stone, metal,
3.2 × 2.1 cm
Inv. 2012.48.1908

12. François Hugo
Button, 1941
Set stone, metal,
4.3 × 5.5 cm
Inv. 2012.48.1904

Musée des Arts Décoratifs, Paris, formerly Loïc Allio collection
Purchased thanks to the Fonds du Patrimoine et au Mécénat, 2012

13.

14.

15.

16.

13. Jean Schlumberger
Angel clips, 1937
Gilt bronze,
6.3 × 3.5 cm
Collection Mark Walsh Leslie Chin, Vintage Luxury, New York

14. Jean Schlumberger
Hand clip, 1938
Gilt bronze,
8 × 4 cm
Collection Mark Walsh Leslie Chin, Vintage Luxury, New York

15. Jean Schlumberger
Roi Soleil clip, 1937
Silver-plated bronze,
Diam. 5.2 cm
Collection Mark Walsh Leslie Chin, Vintage Luxury, New York

16. Jean Schlumberger
Clip, 1937–39
Gilt metal, enamel, glass,
3.3 × 6 cm
Musée des Arts Décoratifs, Paris, anonymous gift, 1996
Inv. 996.65.8

17. Jean Schlumberger
Button, 1937–40
Gilt metal, enamel,
1.8 × 1.5 cm
Musée des Arts Décoratifs, Paris, anonymous gift, 1996
Inv. 996.65.11.19

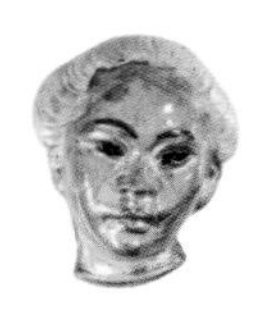

17.

18.

19.

20.

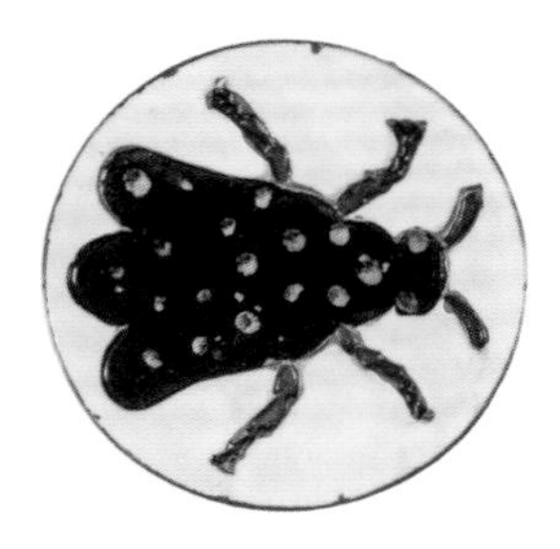

21.

18. Jean Schlumberger
Button, 1938–40
Gilt metal, enamel,
Diam. 2.5 cm
Musée des Arts Décoratifs,
Paris, anonymous gift, 1996
Inv. 996.65.11.26

19. Jean Schlumberger
Clip, 1938
Gilt and enameled metal,
5.1 × 4.5 cm
Musée des Arts Décoratifs,
Paris, anonymous gift, 1996
Inv. 996.65.9.1

20. Jean Schlumberger
Comb, 1937–39
Gilt and enameled metal,
10.2 × 2.5 cm
Musée des Arts Décoratifs,
Paris, anonymous gift, 1996
Inv. 996.65.4.1

21. Jean Schlumberger
Button, 1937–39
Gilt metal, enamel,
Diam. 3.5 cm
Musée des Arts Décoratifs,
Paris, anonymous gift, 1996
Inv. 996.65.11.11

THE DESIGN DRAWINGS

The Schiaparelli Collection: A Legacy of Drawings

Elsa Schiaparelli's 1973 gift to Ufac included 6,387 design drawings dating from 1933 to 1953, in 55 bound albums or loose, which are now in the Musée des Arts Décoratifs. Unsigned, the drawings were made using graphite pencil, colored pencil, ink, felt-tip pen, watercolor, and gouache on drawing paper. Immediately after the collection was presented in the designer's couture salons, illustrators employed by Maison Schiaparelli rapidly and precisely drew the models wearing the outfits. Every garment's shape and volume were highlighted, and hats, gloves, and jewelry completed each look. Unlike the sketches by illustrators in fashion magazines, these drawings were not meant to be published. Along with the program given to the show's guests indicating the collection's theme and trends, these drawings provided technical information and were also promotional tools—clients who could not attend the show would be able to place orders. Considered documentary and not artistic reproductions, these drawings, with their colors and precise details, faithfully reproduce the garments from all angles (usually the front and back). Fabric samples were sometimes glued to the pages.

The drawings thus constitute precise, essential records of numerous Schiaparelli designs over twenty or so years, following the rhythm of four annual collections: spring, summer, fall, and winter. They capture the rich variations and power of seduction still so vibrant in Elsa Schiaparelli's creations.

M.-S.C.C.

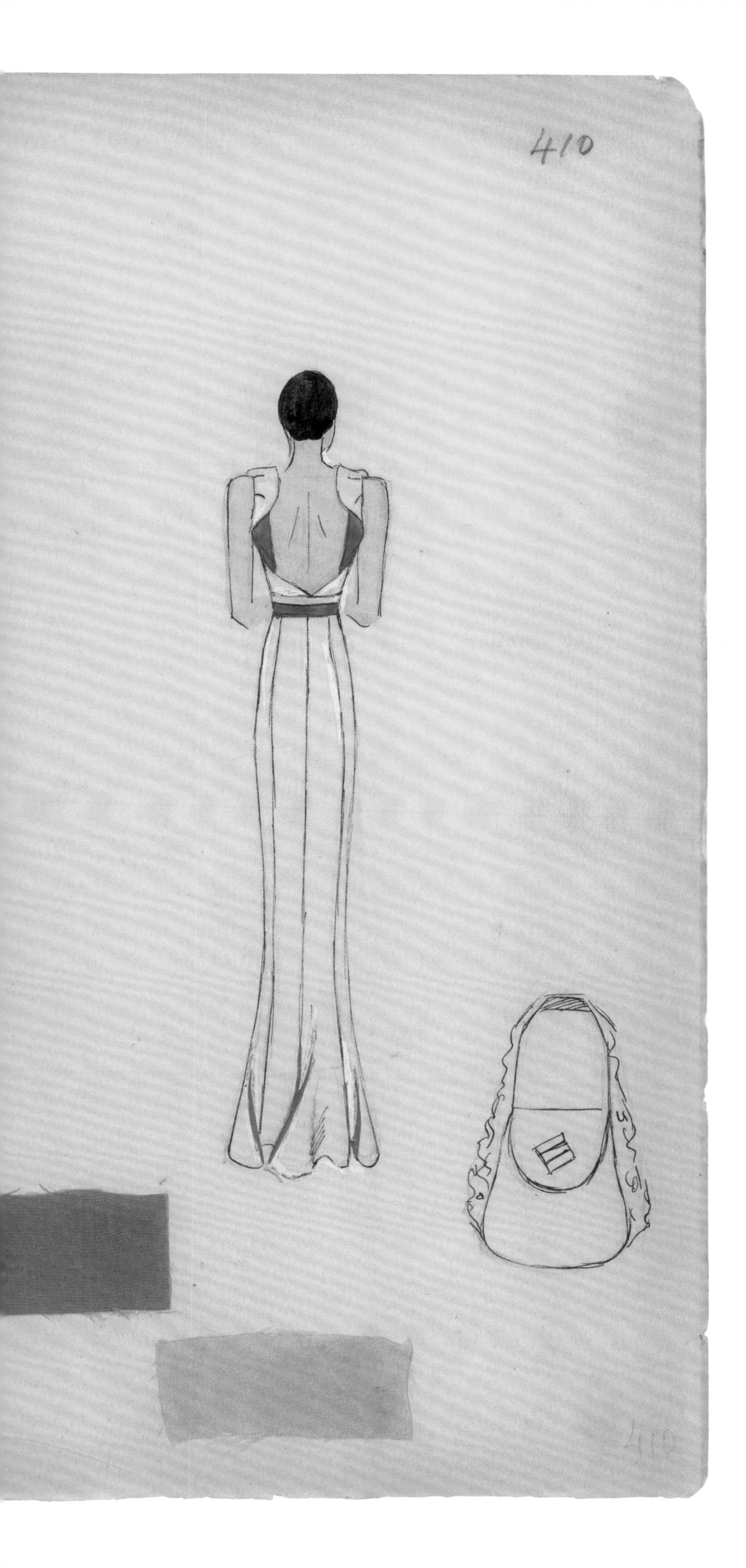

Design drawing, dress and cape, winter 1933–34. Musée des Arts Décoratifs, Paris, gift of Elsa Schiaparelli, Ufac, 1973, inv. UF D 73-21-233.

78

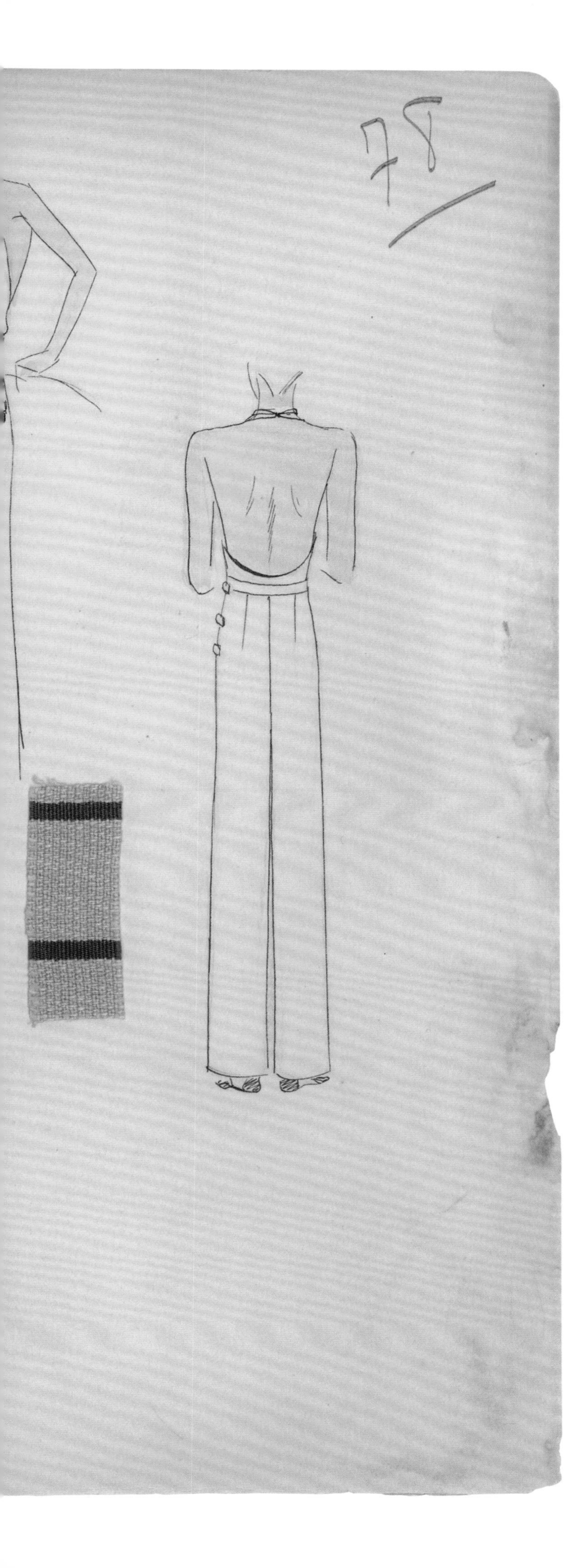

Design drawing, beach pyjamas, pants, bodice, summer or fall 1933. Musée des Arts Décoratifs, Paris, gift of Elsa Schiaparelli, Ufac, 1973, inv. UF D 73-21-352.

Design drawing, hats, summer 1935.
Musée des Arts Décoratifs, Paris,
gift of Elsa Schiaparelli, Ufac, 1973,
inv. UF D 73-21-647.

Design drawing, evening dress, summer 1937. Musée des Arts Décoratifs, Paris, gift of Elsa Schiaparelli, Ufac, 1973, inv. UF D 73-21-1582.

116

Design drawing, cape and evening dress, spring 1937. Musée des Arts Décoratifs, Paris, gift of Elsa Schiaparelli, Ufac, inv. UF D 73-21-1327.

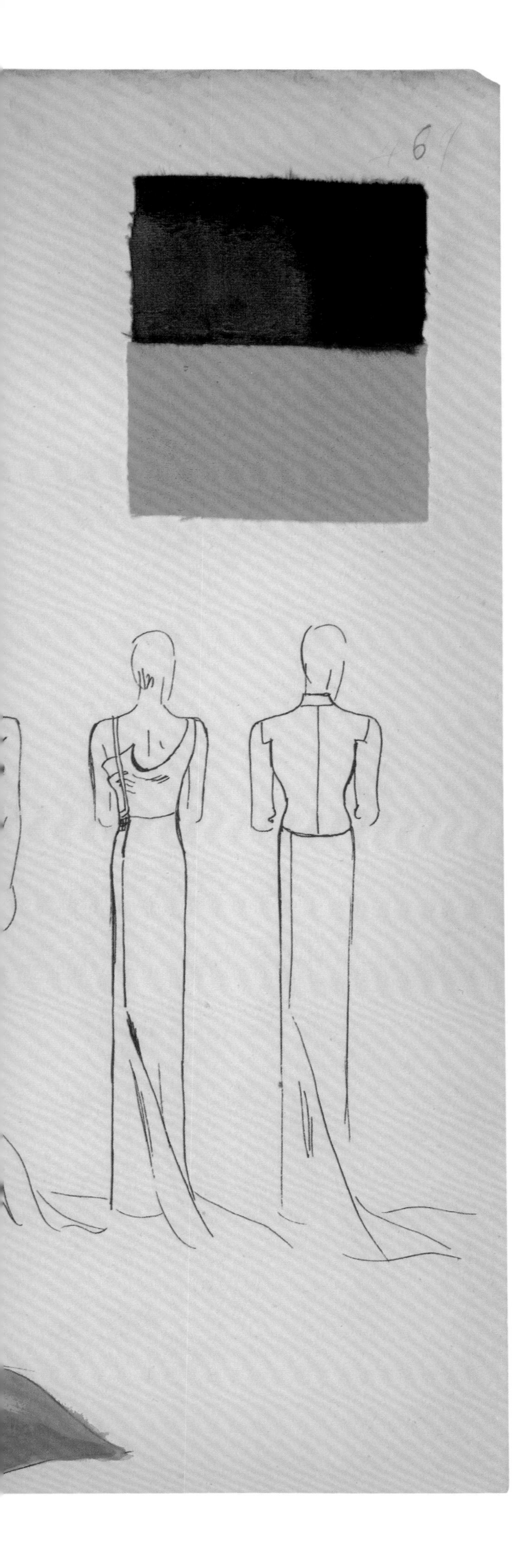

Design drawing, jacket and evening dress, winter 1937–38. Musée des Arts Décoratifs, Paris, gift of Elsa Schiaparelli, Ufac, 1973, inv. UF D 73-21-1421.

Design drawing, hats, summer 1938.
Musée des Arts Décoratifs, Paris,
gift of Elsa Schiaparelli, Ufac, 1973,
inv. UF D 73-21-1748.

4

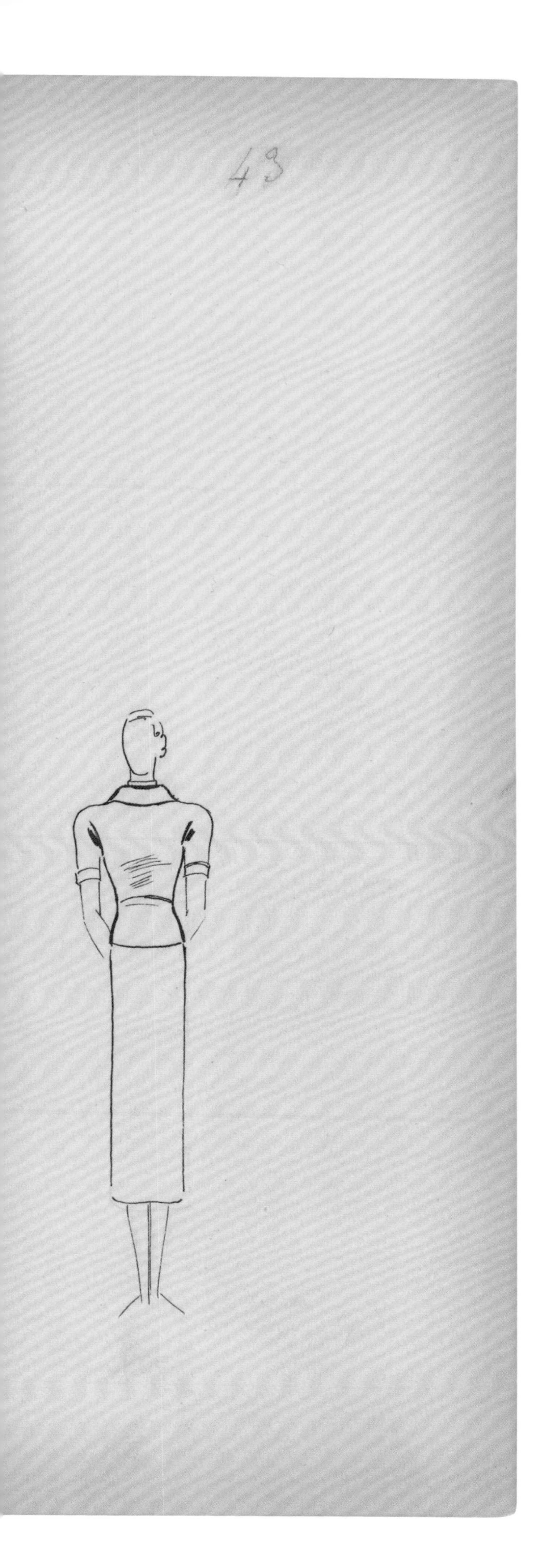

Design drawing, jacket, skirt, summer 1938. Musée des Arts Décoratifs, Paris, gift of Elsa Schiaparelli, Ufac, 1973, inv. UF D 73-21-1796.

Design drawing, evening dress, scarf, summer 1938. Musée des Arts Décoratifs, Paris, gift of Elsa Schiaparelli, Ufac, 1973, inv. UF D 73-21-1826.

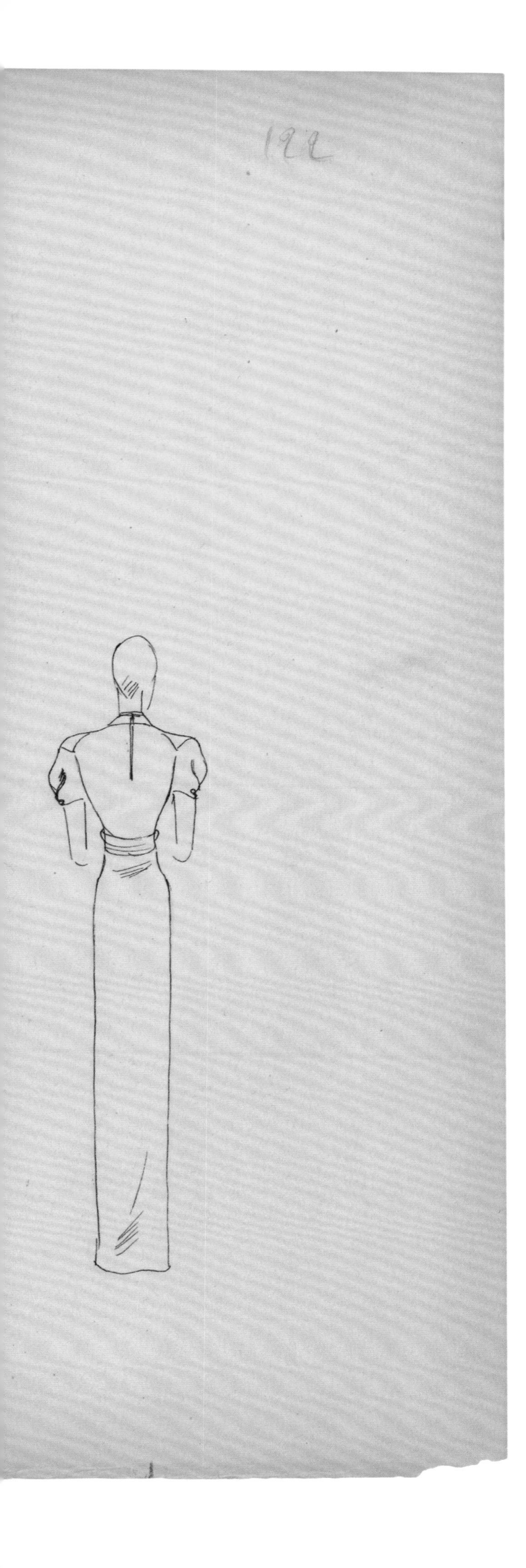

Design drawing, evening dress, summer 1938. Musée des Arts Décoratifs, Paris, gift of Elsa Schiaparelli, Ufac, 1973, inv. UF D 73-21-1873.

Design drawing, jacket, dress, gloves, summer 1938. Musée des Arts Décoratifs, Paris, gift of Elsa Schiaparelli, Ufac, 1973, inv. UF D 73-21-2117.

Design drawing, hats, fall 1939.
Musée des Arts Décoratifs, Paris,
gift of Elsa Schiaparelli, Ufac, 1973,
inv. UF D 73-21-2286 bis.

Design drawing, ski suit, spring 1940. Musée des Arts Décoratifs, Paris, gift of Elsa Schiaparelli, Ufac, 1973, inv. UF D 73-21-2391.

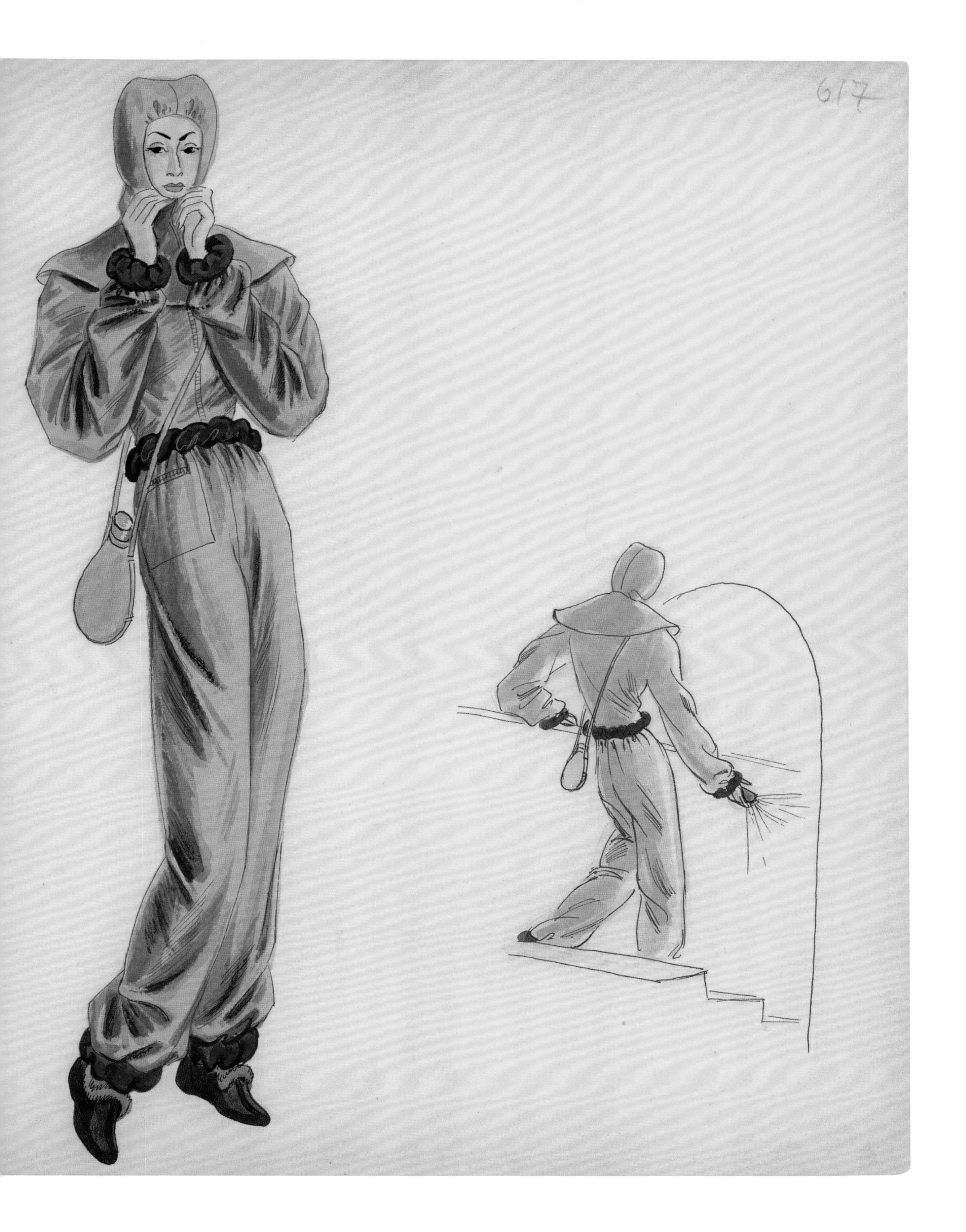
617

Design drawing, evening dress, fall 1947. Musée des Arts Décoratifs, Paris, gift of Elsa Schiaparelli, Ufac, 1973, inv. UF D 73-21-3932.

Design drawing, dress and coats, spring 1951. Musée des Arts Décoratifs, Paris, gift of Elsa Schiaparelli, Ufac, 1973, inv. UF D 73-21-4938.

634-

Design drawing, evening dress, summer 1951. Musée des Arts Décoratifs, Paris, gift of Elsa Schiaparelli, Ufac, 1973, inv. UF D 73-21-5187.

1051

SCHIAPARELLI TODAY

More Beautiful When Broken: A Conversation with Daniel Roseberry

Hanya Yanagihara

Anyone who loves an artist knows that, when you do, you love not one person, but two: the person who makes the work, and the person he is when he's not working. Although perhaps that's unfair; after all, when is an artist not working? So maybe the more accurate way of phrasing it is that you love the performer (because virtually every artist is a performer in some sense, literally or otherwise), and you also love the person he is when the curtain falls.

I am profoundly lucky to be witness to Daniel Roseberry in many guises: The person on stage, yes, giving interviews and overseeing his presentations and shows; but also the person in the atelier, creating with his team; the person on vacation, diving into a cold blue sea; and the person at home, cooking himself a late dinner and talking to me on the phone—he calling from Paris, me answering in New York—every night, in one of the fluid, expansive, sometimes serious, sometimes silly conversations we have that are equal parts pep talks and commiserations, and are as much about our respective creative projects as they are about ourselves, and the orbits we move through, together and separately.

Anyone who loves an artist also knows that you can feel one way about your friend's work and another way about your friend's *true* work, which is being a person in the world. And here, too, I am profoundly lucky, for not only do I admire Daniel in both realms, but he has allowed me the opportunity to watch his collections develop, to let me see the fragile, vulnerable process by which an idea makes the difficult journey from his mind to the page to the dress form. As an artist myself, albeit in a different medium, I know that there are few greater acts of generosity and trust than this.

I think people who know Daniel only through his designs are always surprised by how humble the man himself is, how guileless, how unassuming. His work is so powerful, so emphatic, so bold, that seeing it, you expect the person behind it to be as declarative. Yet if you look closely, you'll see that the gap between who he is and what he makes isn't so wide after all—both are defined by a sense of wonder, an innocence, an emotional depth and breadth. They are rare qualities, in both fashion and in humans, and they are his. May he—and may we—have them forever.

Hanya Yanagihara

H.Y. Hi, my dear Daniel. I always say that the most unfair question you can ask an artist—especially a visual artist—is where your ideas come from. It's such a lazy question, and such an unsatisfying one, both for the interviewer and for the subject, because so much of inspiration is inarticulable. Then there's the fact that what's inspirational to an artist at any given time is not necessarily a big idea or concept: It's a detail, something incidental and often overlooked.

Schiaparelli Haute Couture spring-summer 2021. Hand-painted bustier made from natural calfskin and moulded from a custom sculpture, fastened with corset lacing at the back. Long black crepe skirt affixed with an oversize bow in shocking pink satin silk. Maison Schiaparelli.

SCHIAPARELLI

So, I'm going to ask instead about another important element in an artist's process: Fantasy. I often feel that my most fertile creative periods are ones in which I can drift into a prolonged state of daydreaming. How much has fantasy—either the act of dreaming, or, more literally, influences like *Dune*—influenced your designs, and how central is it in your life?

D.R. I think when I was younger I had a real problem with the amount of daydreaming I was doing. Even in my twenties, daydreaming was overrunning my life and keeping me from doing the things I was actually dreaming of doing.

Once, when I was still a sort of sexually frustrated closeted kid in my early twenties, I went to see a therapist. After about six months of treatment, he said to me, "Daniel, you have such a beautiful fantasy life—but you're much better in reality. Try to stay in reality more." That simple suggestion changed my life. I started to reimagine how I spent my mental time. I was still daydreaming, yes, but I began spending more time trying to make those dreams come true. It was a big shift for me.

And now, ten years later, here we are at Schiaparelli in Paris on the Place Vendôme. Just being here is a dream fulfilled. The catch, though, is that these days, it requires so much more energy to simply daydream like I used to: to forget about all of the pressures and the realities of what it means to work in this industry, to drift away into somewhere more innocent, more childlike.

As an adult, daydreaming requires some level of discipline. You have to fight for it more. It feels like a real luxury now.

Bella Hadid in Schiaparelli Haute Couture fall-winter 2021–22.
Maison Schiaparelli.

Schiaparelli Haute Couture fall-winter 2021–22.
Long sleeve dress in wool crepe with a low-cut neckline, and a gilded necklace in the shape of trompe l'oeil lungs adorned with rhinestones.
Maison Schiaparelli.

SCHIAPARELLI

Secret purse, Schiaparelli haute couture, spring-summer 2022.
Secret bag in gold leather with padlock clasp, with two gold-plated brass feet. It is adorned with jewels, with two differently colored eyes in printed resin giving the illusion of a face.
Maison Schiaparelli.

Schiaparelli Haute Couture fall-winter 2021–22.
Patchwork embroidery with Elsa Schiaparelli's original Lesage swatches
Golden strass, pearls, rhinestones, lurex thread.
3D printed golden nipples, ears, mouths, and noses.
Maison Schiaparelli.

H.Y. I know someone we both admire once said to you: Dreams are expensive. What does that mean for you?

D.R. I sort of feel like dreams choose you. You have a dream, and you have a choice. You either pursue the dream to the end, sacrificing comfort and quiet, putting yourself on the line, moving to strange cities in foreign countries. But you do it all to pursue what the dream has told you could be possible. On the other hand, you could always choose to let the dream go—and maybe there's a beautiful life on the other side of that as well.

H.Y. I always like to ask artists what question they never want to be asked again; you've said that yours would be "Who is the Schiaparelli woman?" Will you tell me why you're sick of that question? Is the idea of imagining "the woman" a retrograde concept in this age?

D.R. I think so. I think the whole dynamic of a man putting women in clothes can start to feel like he's dressing a doll or something. Of course, this doesn't apply to all male designers, but I've never really been motivated or inspired by fetishizing this idea of an ideal woman. For me, it's more about creating an emotion. Whether that's by serving a client who has ordered something special for some key event in her life, or putting on a show for hundreds of people.

[The designer and former artistic director of Celine] Phoebe Philo changed everything. Yes, her aesthetic influence was so strong. But it was the fact that she was a woman that made her a game changer. There have been amazing female designers throughout history, but Phoebe created a ripple effect in fashion that we haven't seen since the days of Coco Chanel and Elsa Schiaparelli herself. She shifted something in the industry forever.

H.Y. I always think that one of the things that distinguishes your work is how powerfully it conveys emotion—and you, in your personal life, are also unafraid of being emotionally expressive. You can very easily access a wide range of feelings, from sorrow to—wonderfully—joy (I don't call you Giggles for nothing).

SCHIAPARELLI

This is reductive, but if we think of designers as either cerebral or intuitive, I consider you largely intuitive. Do you think that's a fair assessment? How do you assess the designers you admire, like Alexander McQueen or Yves Saint Laurent? What does it mean to be "emotional" in your designs?

Schiaparelli Haute Couture fall-winter 2021–22. Filigree lamella thread, pearls, cut beads, handmade pompoms, Swarovski rhinestones, and strass. Trompe l'oeil golden nipples Gazelle horns on an artisanal metal structure. Maison Schiaparelli.

D.R. Do you think my work conveys emotion? I mean, coming from you, the master manipulator of human emotion, that means something!
I do think every designer has to choose a lane. And I think when it works it's because the work and the lane are consistent with who the designer really is. When you sense the designer is trying to be somebody else, or trying to be an elevated version of themselves, the work itself tends to be less powerful. The designers I admire, like McQueen and Yves and Karl Lagerfeld, were all making work that in some way harmoniously and truthfully reflected who they really were: The romantic. The genius. The showman.

H.Y. Some of your most powerful and signature designs play with the idea of anatomical displacements and exaggerations: noses migrate to earlobes, nipples make their way into chokers, breasts take on pyramidal proportions. How much of this (or how little) is a projection of your own relationship with your body?

D.R. That's a great question. It wasn't until around thirty that I started to really embrace and befriend my own body.
There's something inexpressibly glorious about the human body. For one, in the fact that we all have one: we all have ears, we all have a nose. There's also something universally unsettling about seeing your own body reflected back at you. In my designs, I try to treat all body parts with some level of democracy. Breasts are considered as precious as eyes, toes are as sexy as your ass. It's a way of glorifying the body without oversexualizing it.

H.Y. Talk to me about what it's like to both create within a legacy —that of Madame Schiaparelli—while, at the same time, making something of your own. Does the ghost of Elsa ever feel oppressive, or do you feel you have a balanced relationship with her?

D.R. At the beginning of my time here at Schiaparelli I really didn't focus on her work. Or rather, not the specifics of her work. I was trying to elicit the same emotional response that you might have had during her lifetime, looking at her work. That was the brief I gave to myself.

But now, a few years into this tenure here, I feel much more at ease with her legacy and the archives, and more inclined to embrace certain parts of them with each season. But I've never felt oppressed by her legacy, though I've also always kept it at arm's length. There are people who are guardians of her memory, experts in her life, and scholars of her achievements—of which there are many. But that's not really my role. I kind of had this image of her passing the torch. I don't think she would be interested in seeing her work reissued over and over again, a century later. I think she would be championing the new, and I can only hope that that would include me.

H.Y. What is the point and purpose of a dress in 2022? Traditionally, it's a gendered piece of clothing, one women are no longer expected to wear, but instead choose to wear. Will you talk about your philosophy (if you have one) about what a dress should be and do?

D.R. I think there's a reason why the dress is a forever piece, and it's the same reason why the suit is also timeless. It's because it was designed to amplify the most beautiful parts of a woman's body, and also create some ease around the parts of the body that sometimes need a helping hand. I think a great dress is defined by how generous it is. How much

SCHIAPARELLI

Schiaparelli Haute Couture fall-winter 2021. Mini dress with corset lacing in the back. Hand embroidered pink silk taffeta roses. Black wool crepe and duchess satin. Maison Schiaparelli.

Lady Gaga in custom Schiaparelli Haute Couture for her performance of the American national anthem at the inauguration of President Joe Biden. Maison Schiaparelli.

Daniel Roseberry, digital collage of Lady Gaga's dress for her performance of the American national anthem at the inauguration of President Joe Biden. Maison Schiaparelli

confidence does it give you? How much glamour can it bring to your life, to your evening, to your Sunday morning? Does it serve you? And does it serve the moment for which it is worn?

All that being said, dresses can look incredible on men, and suits can look absolutely stunning on women. I think we're seeing today that these rules about dressing are even more beautiful when they're broken.

H.Y. The term "surreal" gets tossed around a lot these days as a short hand for anything that seems absurd, ridiculous, or strange. And yet the word, as defined by the writer André Breton in 1924, meant something specific: the space between the dream life and the real one, and the struggle to settle them. But what does the term mean to you, and how does that belief express itself in your designs?

D.R. This might be a frustrating answer but I think, for me, surrealism exists in the space between two extremes. Something that is between fantasy and reality, something that's between darkness and light. The refusal to be either one is indicative of surreal work.

I also think it has to arouse some level of curiosity in the viewer. I find that there's this curious response to so much of surreal work I've seen or made: It makes you feel *something*, but it's not completely clear what, or why. In this way, it's different from romantic work or modernist work. The surreal feels just out of reach, but its emotional punch is visceral and sometimes even urgent. Maybe that's what Breton meant when he speaks of the struggle to settle two opposing realities. We always talk about contradiction in the studio: how can we make something baroque and minimal at the same time, for example. We want something both male and female, soft and hard, pop and couture. The two extremes need each other, and on top of that, they want each other, too.

H.Y. Let's talk more broadly about the fashion world and industry, which we've discussed many times over the years. I always say that there's perhaps no other business in which the gap between the perceived glamor of the job and its daily reality is wider. Is that dissonance ever difficult for you to navigate?

D.R. This is something that's on my mind and something that I have to navigate every day—or maybe every other day. There are days, really beautiful days, when fashion *does* feel like the fantasy that you always thought it would be. Sometimes, when we fit the couture all day long, it just feels like Christmas morning for grown-ups, but even better because we're creating together.

But those days are not the majority of days, and accepting this has been something that I think anyone who works in fashion, and maybe especially anyone who is a designer, has to reckon with. For me, the hardest part is the rate at which you're expected to come up with ideas worth sharing with the world. Social media has made this even more demanding, even more relentless, and I think that's why there's so much fluffy fashion out there—it's simply not possible for the same team or the same designer to create magical, earth-shattering ideas en masse, four times a year.

I've told you this so many times, but I'm always so envious of writers, and musicians, and actors, because the rate at which they have to create their work feels so much more civilized to me. There are explosive moments of hyper creativity—and then there are moments where you're allowed to disappear, and to recharge, and to fill yourself back up. In other industries, those periods could last for years. But in fashion, you get two weeks between collections, if any at all. If you take off any more than two weeks, you're already behind.

The glamorous facade of the industry feels necessary. It's what draws people in, and it's what people want it to be. But that glamor is also the exception that proves the rule.

H.Y. Before you arrived at the *maison* in 2019, you had worked at the American brand Thom Browne for ten years, eventually rising to become the design director for both the men's and women's collections.

You mentioned that you've noticed that young people these days hope to go directly from design school to helming their own brand. Yet, you've always said, there are good reasons to be the number two at a fashion house. Tell me about them, and what you learned from your years at Thom Browne.

Schiaparelli Haute Couture spring-summer 2022. Vintage cabochons, rhinestones, and jewels. Hand-molded embroidered leather in the shape of the motifs of Schiaparelli. Maison Schiaparelli.

D.R. The first thing I realized at Thom Browne was that I really didn't know anything at all. Which meant that I made a lot of mistakes—and fortunately, I had Thom to protect me from those mistakes, and to mentor and to train me.

There are so many different ways to mess up in this industry. There are all of the professional ways: The missed opportunities, the overexposure or the underexposure, and all of the relentless, unforgiving realities of lead times and delivery windows and sell-throughs and all of that. But more importantly, there's the chance you'll blow your chance to become the person that you're meant to become.

I've always felt like it's a very dangerous place to be in, to be a young person learning about who they are, or rather, who they're becoming, while also being expected to deal with the pressures of the industry. Some people really are built for it—I, on the other hand, will be forever grateful that I was a number two for over a decade. The one thing that I don't think that you learn as a number two is what your own process will look like when you're out on your own. When I started at Schiaparelli, I had to unlearn some things about the way I'd learned to work and figure out how to tap into my own vision: My own way of working and my own way of building a collection. This can be really traumatic to do in public. But it's also a necessary part of the process. All you can ask for is patience—from the industry and, more importantly, from yourself.

H.Y. Soon after we met, you said that you approached design "with a servant's heart": I thought it was such a beautiful expression, and of course one that comes from the Christian faith in which you were raised.

Will you talk about what you meant by that? What is the relationship between the designer and the person who wears his clothes? How much has your faith informed your approach to being a designer?

D.R. I've always felt like being a designer was being in the service industry. At the end of the day, this isn't a pure art—this is an applied art, one that we offer in service to people who care about what we do.

I can no longer ascribe to the narrow and exclusionary parts of Christianity, but what it did teach me is that there is power and strength in serving others. It taught me that giving yourself away, being generous with the gifts that have been given to you, with your time, actually gives you strength in return.

It's the opposite of how the culture at large thinks about who a fashion designer is. And it's been a true joy to meet many of my fellow designers and many of the people that I've long admired in this industry—because in reality, they aren't who they seem to be. I think the industry is filled with people who probably weren't the coolest kids growing up. But now they're making their way, and in doing so, they're creating culture: one dress, one shoe, one show at a time.

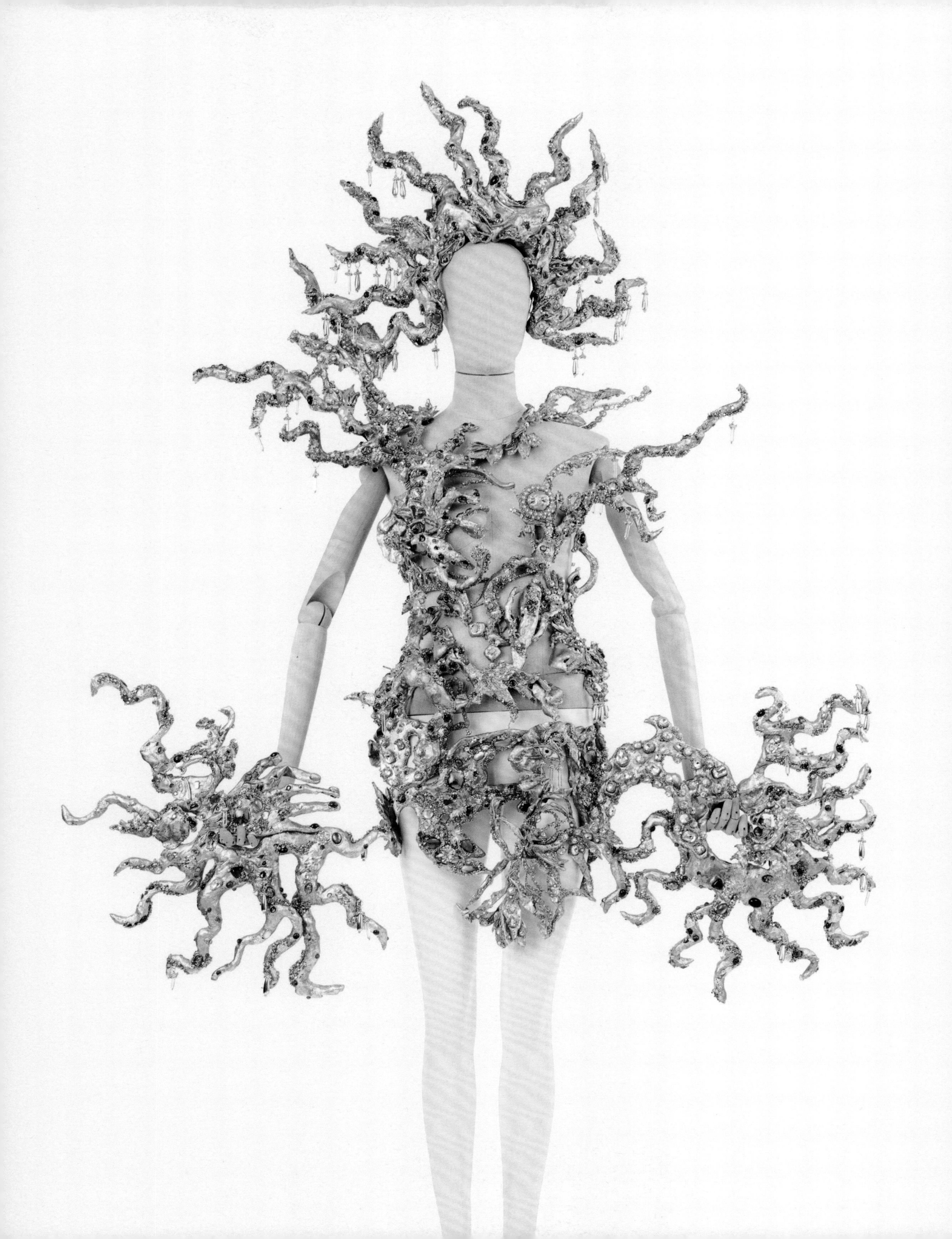

APPENDICES

Clothing and Accessories from the Musée des Arts Décoratifs de Paris Collection

Sweater
1928
→ p. 70

Wool knit

Purchased, 2005
Inv. 2005-39-1

Hat
1930–33

Metallic knit

Gift of Elsa Schiaparelli, Ufac, 1973
Inv. UF 73-21-88

Apron
Spring 1935
→ p. 74

Rhodophane by Colcombet, crepe de chine, taffeta, and coated canvas

Gift of Elsa Schiaparelli, Ufac, 1973
Inv. UF 73-21-53

Evening cape
Summer 1935
→ p. 78

Simoun crinkle taffeta by Bianchini-Férier

Gift of Elinor Brodie, Ufac, 1969
Inv. UF 69-28-18

Pair of fingerless gloves
c. 1936

Kid leather

Gift of Elsa Schiaparelli, Ufac, 1973
Inv. UF 73-21-75 AB

Pair of gloves
Winter 1936–37
→ p. 82

Suede

Gift of Elsa Schiaparelli, Ufac, 1973
Inv. UF 73-21-77 AB

Evening jacket
Winter 1936–37
→ p. 86

Wool embroidered with lamellae and sequins by Lesage

Gift of Patricia López-Willshaw, Ufac, 1966
Inv. UF 66-38-10

Dress
Winter 1936–37

Silk jersey embroidered with sequins, filés, and lamellae

Gift of Lila de Nobili, Ufac, 1969
Inv. UF 69-1-3

Evening bolero
Summer 1937

Silk satin, embroidery, and appliqué cordonnets, tube beads, and glass leaves and flowers

Gift of Patricia López-Willshaw, Ufac, 1966
Inv. 66-38-13

Evening jacket
Summer 1937
→ p. 90

Wool, Rhodoid buttons

Gift of Patricia López-Willshaw, Ufac, 1966
Inv. UF 66-38-11

Evening dress
Summer 1937
→ p. 94

Printed silk crepe

Gift of Monsieur Perrigot, Ufac, 1950
Inv. UF 50-17-12

Evening outfit
Summer 1937
→ p. 98

Printed silk satin, silk crepe, filet by Ducharne

Gift of Patricia López-Willshaw, Ufac, 1966
Inv. 66-38-4 AB

Evening jacket
Winter collection, 1937–38

Wool, embroidered with lamellae, filés, beads, and claw-set, painted rhinestones

Gift of Patricia López-Willshaw, Ufac, 1966
Inv. UF 66-38-12

Pair of fingerless gloves
Winter 1937–38

Wool, wool embroidery

Gift of Patricia López-Willshaw, Ufac, 1966
Inv. 66-38-66 AB

Evening jacket
Spring 1938
→ p. 102

Silk velvet, embroidered with lamellae, cannetilles, and claw-set stones by Lesage, molded resin buttons with embedded flowers

Gift of Elsa Schiaparelli, Ufac, 1973
Inv. UF 73-21-68

Jacket
Spring 1938

Silk corduroy, resin buttons

Gift of Elsa Schiaparelli, Ufac, 1973
Inv. UF 73-21-55

Evening dress
Spring 1938

Black silk crepe with smocking/pleating, appliqué sequins and lamellae

Purchased, Ufac, 1988
Inv. UF 88-11-1

Jacket
Summer 1938

Wool, silk satin, embroidery by Lesage

Gift of Elsa Schiaparelli, Ufac, 1973
Inv. UF 73-21-38

Jacket
Summer 1938

Wool, embroidered with beads, stones, rhinestones, filés, and lamellae by Lesage

Gift of Elsa Schiaparelli, Ufac, 1973
Inv. UF 73-21-46

Evening bolero
Summer 1938
→ p. 106

Silk braid embroidery on silk crepe, embroidered with silk thread, ties, cabochons, beads, and mirrors by Lesage

Gift of Elsa Schiaparelli, Ufac, 1973
Inv. UF 73-21-48

Evening bolero
Summer 1938
→ p. 110

Silk satin, passementerie, appliqué ties, silk chenille, lamella, rhinestone, and sequin embroidery by Lesage

Gift of Elsa Schiaparelli, Ufac, 1973
Inv. UF 73-21-50

Evening jacket
Summer 1938

Wool, silk crepe, purl appliqués by Lesage, resin buttons

Gift of Elsa Schiaparelli, Ufac, 1973
Inv. UF 73-21-64

Pair of sandals
André Perugia for Padova
Made for Elsa Schiaparelli
Summer 1938

Kid, suede with gold kid piping

Gift of Patricia López-Willshaw, Ufac, 1966
Inv. UF 66-38-52 AB

Pair of sandals
André Perugia for Padova
Made for Elsa Schiaparelli
Summer 1938

Kid, suede with gold kid piping

Gift of Patricia López-Willshaw, Ufac, 1966
Inv. UF 66-38-54 AB

Veil
Summer 1938

Silk tulle, glass tube bead embroidery by Lesage

Gift of Elsa Schiaparelli, Ufac, 1973
Inv. UF 73-21-51

Evening cape
Summer 1938

Silk moiré, silk velvet, passementerie

Gift of Elsa Schiaparelli, Ufac, 1973
Inv. UF 73-21-16

Pair of fingerless gloves
Summer 1938

Silk satin, painted metal buttons

Gift of Elsa Schiaparelli, Ufac, 1973
Inv. UF 73-21-73 AB

Jacket
Fall 1938
→ p. 114

Rayon crepe, moiré, painted metal insects by Jean Schlumberger

Gift of Elsa Schiaparelli, Ufac, 1973
Inv. UF 73-21-70

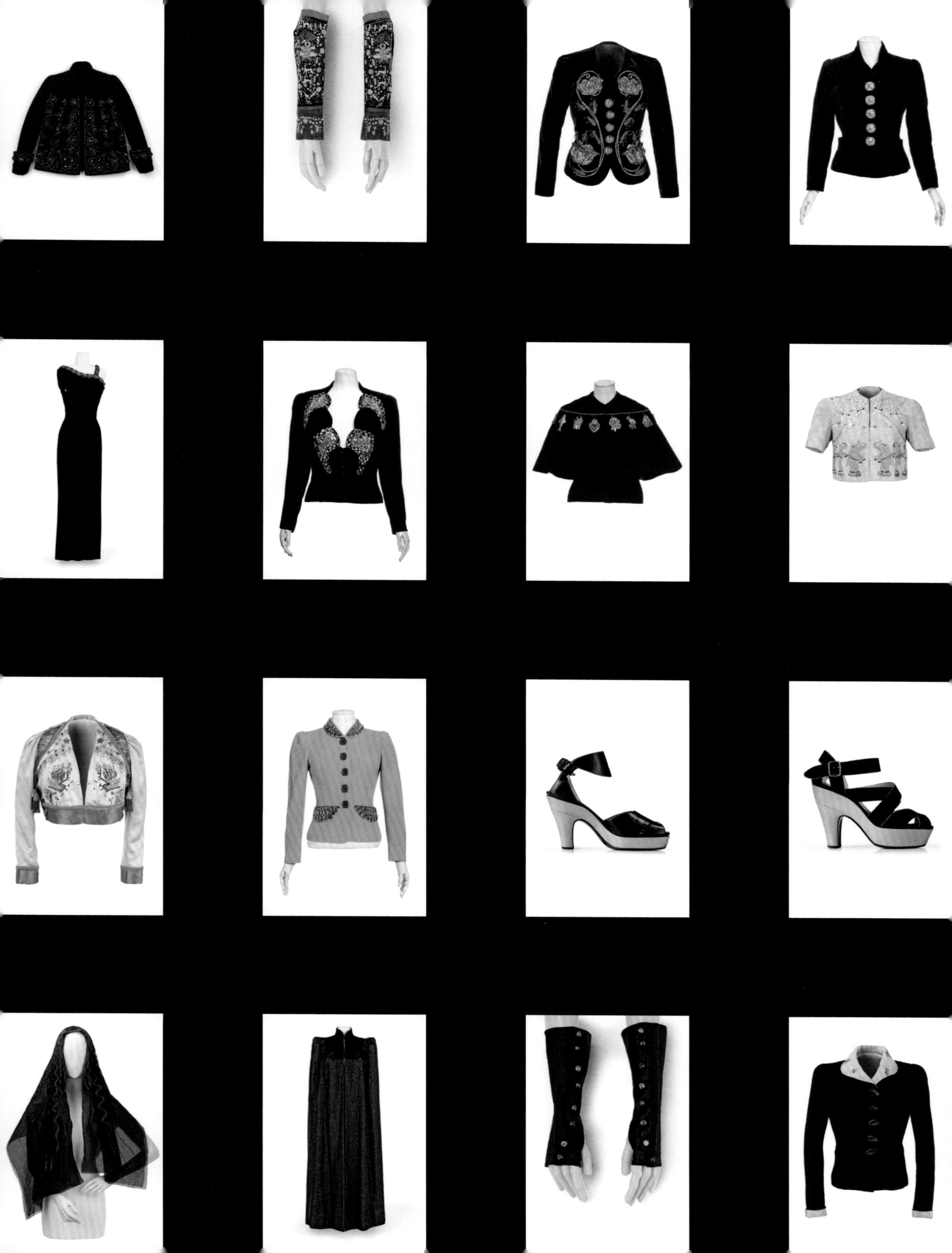

Evening cape
Fall 1938
→ p. 118

Silk organdy, goffered silk taffeta, glass tube bead embroidery

Gift of Patricia López-Willshaw, Ufac, 1966
Inv. UF 66-38-14

Evening jacket
Fall 1938

Silk satin, tinsel, rhinestone, and cabochon embroidery

Gift of Elsa Schiaparelli, Ufac, 1973
Inv. UF 73-21-57

Evening dress
Fall collection, 1938

Silk jersey embroidered with filés, lamellae, and cabochons, laurel wreath appliqués

Gift of Elsa Schiaparelli, Ufac, 1973
Inv. UF 73-21-3

Evening cape
Fall 1938

Silk organza, embroidered with beads, stones, silk cord and tassel

Gift of Elsa Schiaparelli, Ufac, 1973
Inv. UF 73-21-45

Evening dress
Fall 1938
→ p. 122

Silk crepe, silk and metallic thread embroidery by Lesage, appliqué flower and leaf garlands in coated canvas

Gift of Elsa Schiaparelli, Ufac, 1973
Inv. UF 73-21-7

Evening jacket
Winter 1938–39

Silk faille, silk thread embroidery by Lesage

Gift of Patricia López-Willshaw, Ufac, 1966
Inv. 66-38-9

Evening dress
Winter 1938–39

Silk crepe, taffeta, glass tube bead embroidery

Gift of Elsa Schiaparelli, Ufac, 1973
Inv. UF 73-21-34

Jacket
Winter 1938–39

Hammered silk velvet, silk thread and bead embroidery by Lesage, painted metal buttons

Gift of Elsa Schiaparelli, Ufac, 1973
Inv. UF 73-21-62

Evening dress
Winter 1938–39
→ p. 126

Ducharne pekin silk

Gift of Patricia López-Willshaw, Ufac, 1966
Inv. 66-38-3

Evening coat
Winter 1938–39
→ p. 130

Wool, silk velvet, silk taffeta, lamella, sequin, and porcelain flower embroidery by Lesage, resin buttons

Gift of Patricia López-Willshaw, Ufac, 1966
Inv. UF 66-38-6

Evening ensemble
Winter 1938–39

Silk velvet, fringed and braided silk tassels

Gift of Lucie Noel, Ufac, 1967
Inv. UF 67-20-1 AB

Dress
Winter 1938–39

Silk crepe, passementerie

Gift of Lila de Nobili, Ufac, 1969
Inv. UF 69-1-2

***Phoebus* evening cape**
Winter 1938–39
→ p. 134

Ratteen, quilted silk crepe, paillette, tinsel, and gold thread embroidery by Lesage, passementerie buttons

Gift of Elsa Schiaparelli, Ufac, 1973
Inv. UF 73-21-39

Pair of ankle boots
André Perugia for Padova
Made for Elsa Schiaparelli
Winter 1938–38

Suede

Gift of Patricia López-Willshaw, Ufac, 1966
Inv. UF 66-38-49 AB

Evening dress
Spring 1939

Silk velvet, tinsel embroidery on felt backing

Gift of Comtesse Diane de Castellane in memory of her mother Florinda Fernandez y Anchorena, 1995
Inv. 995.87.1

Evening dress
Summer 1939
→ p. 138

Ducharne printed satin, drawing by Jean Peltier

Purchase made with the support of Susan Bloomberg, 2018
Inv. 2018-65-1

Pair of long gloves
Summer 1939

Suede, leather

Gift of Elsa Schiaparelli, Ufac, 1973
Inv. UF 73-21-82 AB

Evening ensemble
Fall 1939
→ p. 142

Organza, filé, and bead embroidery by Lesage, painted metal buttons

Gift of Patricia López-Willshaw, Ufac, 1966
Inv. UF 66-38-8 A et UF 66-38-5

Pillbox hat
Fall 1939

Cut-out and coated cloth, grosgrain

Gift of Patricia López-Willshaw, Ufac, 1966
Inv. UF 66-38-38

Evening bodice
Fall 1939

Silk chiffon, embroidered with lamellae, filés, cabochons, beads, and rhinestones by Lesage

Gift of Elsa Schiaparelli, Ufac, 1973
Inv. UF 73-21-52

Evening ensemble
Fall 1939
→ p. 146

Silk satin embroidered with lamellae and metallic threads, appliqué celluloid sequins, metal buttons

Gift of Elsa Schiaparelli, Ufac, 1973
Inv. UF 73-21-27 AB

Evening ensemble
Fall 1939
→ p. 150

Ducharne silk scarf print, painted metal buttons by Jean Schlumberger

Gift of Patricia López-Willshaw, Ufac, 1966
Inv. UF 66-38-2 ABCD

Pair of short gloves
1939

Suede

Gift of Elsa Schiaparelli, Ufac, 1973
Inv. UF 73-21-85 AB

Dressing gown
c. 1939

Silk satin, silk guipure lace

Gift of Elsa Schiaparelli, Ufac, 1973
Inv. UF 73-21-9

Pair of short gloves
1930–39

Leather, tulle

Gift of Elsa Schiaparelli, Ufac, 1973
Inv. UF 73-21-83 AB

Pair of short gloves
1930–39

Cotton canvas, crochet inserts

Gift of Elsa Schiaparelli, Ufac, 1973
Inv. UF 73-21-74 AB

Pair of fingerless gloves
c. 1930–39

Kid

Gift of Elsa Schiaparelli, Ufac, 1973
Inv. UF 73-21-76 AB

Pair of short gloves
1930–39

Silk jersey, sequin and bead embroidery

Gift of Elsa Schiaparelli, Ufac, 1973
Inv. UF 73-21-78 AB

Pair of short gloves
1930–39

Kid

Gift of Elsa Schiaparelli, Ufac, 1973
Inv. UF 73-21-80 AB

Pair of short gloves
1930–39

Kid

Gift of Elsa Schiaparelli, Ufac, 1973
Inv. UF 73-21-81 AB

Jacket
Winter 1939–40

Silk velvet, silk satin, passementerie, resin buttons

Gift of Elsa Schiaparelli, Ufac, 1973
Inv. UF 73-21-63

Evening jacket
Winter 1939–40

Silk velvet with diaper-pattern embroidery, resin buttons

Gift of Elsa Schiaparelli, Ufac, 1973
Inv. UF 73-21-65

Evening dress
Winter 1939–40

Silk moiré, silk velvet, passementerie

Gift of Elsa Schiaparelli, Ufac, 1973
Inv. UF 73-21-10

Evening dress
Winter 1939-40
→ p. 154

Ducharne faconne silk velvet on a satin ground

Gift of Elsa Schiaparelli, Ufac, 1973
Inv. UF 73-21-5

Evening coat
Winter 1939–40
→ p. 158

Faconne silk velvet with satin ground, gold-plated buttons

Gift of Elsa Schiaparelli, Ufac, 1973
Inv. UF 73-21-22

Coat
Spring 1940
→ p. 162

Wool twill, leather and metal buttons

Gift of Patricia López-Willshaw, Ufac, 1966
Inv. UF 66-38-7

Evening coat
Summer 1940

Silk ottoman and moiré, metal buttons

Gift of Elsa Schiaparelli, Ufac, 1973
Inv. UF 73-21-25

Belt
c. 1940

Silk satin, passementerie

Gift of Elsa Schiaparelli, Ufac, 1973
Inv. UF 73-21-87

Evening jacket
Summer 1941

Silk crepe, silk thread, filé, and lamella embroidery by Lesage

Gift of Elsa Schiaparelli, Ufac, 1973
Inv. UF 73-21-69

Hat
Fall 1941

Woven straw, silk twill rib

Gift of Lucie Noel, Ufac, 1971
Inv. UF 71-58-1

Evening jacket
1941

Basketweave wool, silk crepe, filé, lamella, and bead embroidery

Gift of Elsa Schiaparelli, Ufac, 1973
Inv. UF 73-21-61

Evening jacket
Summer 1945

Rayon crepe, wool appliqués embroidered with lamellae, sequins, rhinestones, and filés, glass buttons

Gift of Elsa Schiaparelli, Ufac, 1973
Inv. UF 73-21-58

Evening coat
Summer 1945

Silk satin, lamella embroidery by Lesage

Gift of Elsa Schiaparelli, Ufac, 1973
Inv. UF 73-21-24

Bodice
Summer 1945

Silk satin, lamella embroidery by Lesage

Gift of Elsa Schiaparelli, Ufac, 1973
Inv. UF 73-21-56

Evening dress
c. 1945–46

Silk organza lamé

Gift of Elsa Schiaparelli, Ufac, 1973
Inv. UF 73-21-12

Evening coat
1946

Taffeta

Gift of Elsa Schiaparelli, Ufac, 1973
Inv. UF 73-21-13

Day jacket
Spring 1947

Wool serge, "ES" figured silk crepe, filé and purl embroidery

Gift of Elsa Schiaparelli, Ufac, 1973
Inv. UF 73-21-67

Evening jacket
Spring 1947
→ p. 166

Pekin silk, filé, lamella, and sequin embroidery and appliqués

Gift of Elsa Schiaparelli, Ufac, 1973
Inv. UF 73-21-60

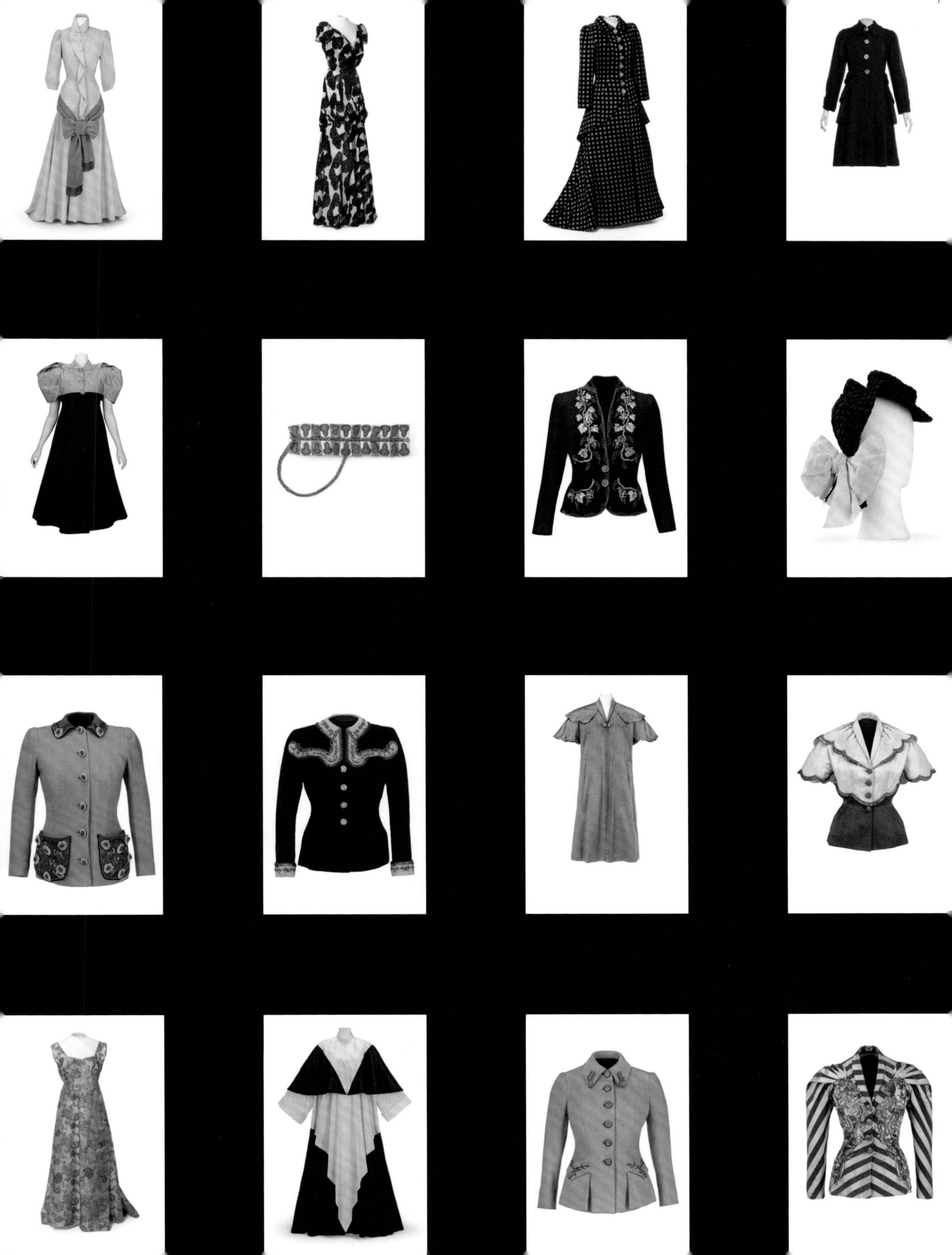

Evening jacket
Spring 1947

Shot, bead and sequin embroidery

Gift of Elsa Schiaparelli, Ufac, 1973
Inv. UF 73-21-59

Pair of short gloves
c. 1947

Silk satin

Gift of Elsa Schiaparelli, Ufac, 1973
Inv. UF 73-21-86 AB

Bodice and skirt ensemble
Summer 1948

Synthetic satin and figured fabric

Gift of Elsa Schiaparelli, Ufac, 1973
Inv. UF 73-21-4 AB

Evening coat
Summer 1948

Taffeta

Gift of Elsa Schiaparelli, Ufac, 1973
Inv. UF 73-21-17

Evening jacket
Summer 1948

Silk velvet and crepe, filé, lamella, and cannetille frogging by Lesage

Gift of Elsa Schiaparelli, Ufac, 1973
Inv. UF 73-21-66

Skirt
Winter 1948–49
→ p. 170

Ducharne pekin taffeta, silk crepe

Gift of Elsa Schiaparelli, Ufac, 1973
Inv. UF 73-21-2

Evening dress
Summer 1949

Embroidered silk organza

Gift of Patricia López-Willshaw, Ufac, 1966
Inv. UF 66-38-19

Bustier
Fall 1949

Taffeta and organdy

Gift of Elsa Schiaparelli, Ufac, 1973
Inv. UF 73-21-71

Evening ensemble
Fall 1949
→ p. 174

Shot taffeta

Gift of Elsa Schiaparelli, Ufac, 1973
Inv. UF 73-21-32

Ankle boots
1949

Woven raffia

Gift of Patricia López-Willshaw, Ufac, 1966
Inv. UF 66-38-57 AB

Evening coat
1945–49

Quilted taffeta

Gift of Elsa Schiaparelli, Ufac, 1973
Inv. UF 73-21-19

Trouser/bodice ensemble
1947–50

Painted cotton velvet, embroidery

Gift of Elsa Schiaparelli, Ufac, 1973
Inv. UF 73-21-26 AB

Evening dress
c. 1948–50

Silk taffeta

Gift of Elsa Schiaparelli, Ufac, 1973
Inv. UF 73-21-8

Evening jacket
Spring 1950
→ p. 178

Silk velvet with braid appliqués and sequined embroidery by Lesage

Gift of Elsa Schiaparelli, Ufac, 1973
Inv. UF 73-21-37

Evening coat
Summer 1950

Shot taffeta, resin buttons

Gift of Elsa Schiaparelli, Ufac, 1973
Inv. UF 73-21-14

Evening coat
Summer 1950

Gros de Tours, resin button

Gift of Elsa Schiaparelli, Ufac, 1973
Inv. UF 73-21-15

Bustier dress
c. 1950

Silk faille

Gift of Elsa Schiaparelli, Ufac, 1973
Inv. UF 73-21-11

Evening dress
Winter 1950–51
→ p. 182

Silk satin, silk velvet, embroidery by Lesage of metallic-thread braid, cordonnet, bead, and rhinestone appliqués

Gift of Elsa Schiaparelli, Ufac, 1973
Inv. UF 73-21-30

Coatdress
Winter 1950–51

Glen paid lamé, buttons by François Hugo

Gift of Madame Saint-Macé, 1986
Inv. 56582

Sports ensemble
1950

White cotton piqué and wool jersey

Gift of Elsa Schiaparelli, Ufac, 1973
Inv. UF 73-21-28 AB

Pair of long gloves
1950

Organza

Gift of Elsa Schiaparelli, Ufac, 1973
Inv. UF 73-21-42 AB

Evening dress
c. 1950

Shantung, bead and metallic-thread embroidery

Gift of Elsa Schiaparelli, Ufac, 1973
Inv. UF 73-21-6

Evening coat
c. 1950

Taffeta

Gift of Elsa Schiaparelli, Ufac, 1973
Inv. UF 73-21-23

Pair of short gloves
c. 1950

Suede

Gift of Elsa Schiaparelli, Ufac, 1973
Inv. UF 73-21-79 AB

Pair of fingerless gloves
c. 1950

Silk satin

Gift of Elsa Schiaparelli, Ufac, 1973
Inv. UF 73-21-44 AB

Evening jacket
Spring 1951
→ p. 186

Silk satin, mink fur appliqués, embroidered with tinsel, rhinestones, tubes, beads, and chenille by Lesage

Gift of Elsa Schiaparelli, Ufac, 1973
Inv. UF 73-21-54

Evening coat
Summer 1951

Silk organza, felt, tube-bead, and silk-thread embroidery

Gift of Elsa Schiaparelli, Ufac, 1973
Inv. UF 73-21-43

Evening dress
Summer 1951

Linen fabric, taffeta, tube-bead fringing

Gift of Elsa Schiaparelli, Ufac, 1973
Inv. UF 73-21-33

Pair of long gloves
Winter 1951–52
→ p. 190

Silk velvet

Gift of Elsa Schiaparelli, Ufac, 1973
Inv. UF 73-21-40 AB

Evening cape
1951

Shot crinkle taffeta by Bianchini-Férier

Gift of Elsa Schiaparelli, Ufac, 1973
Inv. UF 73-21-20

Evening dress
1951

Silk taffeta

Gift of Elsa Schiaparelli, Ufac, 1973
Inv. UF 73-21-29

Evening coat
1951

Quilted, topstitched silk satin

Gift of Elsa Schiaparelli, Ufac, 1973
Inv. UF 73-21-18

Schiap Sport evening dress
Summer 1952

Faille and tulle, silk satin, grosgrain and lace

Gift of Elsa Schiaparelli, Ufac, 1973
Inv. UF 73-21-35 ABCD

Evening coat
Winter 1952–53
→ p. 194

Quilted taffeta decorated with broché velvet

Gift of Elsa Schiaparelli, Ufac, 1973
Inv. UF 73-21-21

Evening dress
Winter 1952–53

Silk satin, taffeta

Gift of Elsa Schiaparelli, Ufac, 1973
Inv. UF 73-21-31

Pair of long gloves
1953

Machine-made cotton lace

Gift of Elsa Schiaparelli, Ufac, 1973
Inv. UF 73-21-41 AB

Pair of long gloves
1950–53

Machine-made cotton lace

Gift of Elsa Schiaparelli, Ufac, 1973
Inv. UF 73-21-84 AB

Long dress
Winter 1953–54

Wool

Gift of Elsa Schiaparelli, Ufac, 1973
Inv. UF 73-21-1

Chronology of the Life of Elsa Schiaparelli

Marie-Sophie Carron de la Carrière

1890

September 10: Elsa Luisa Maria, younger daughter of Maria-Luisa and Celestino Schiaparelli, is born in Rome.
Her older sister Beatrice is seven years older than her. The family lives in an apartment in the Palazzo Corsini, a late Baroque building that housed the Accademia dei Lincei, for which Celestino is the librarian. Founded in the seventeenth century, in part by Galileo, the library contains works on botany, oriental culture, architecture, mathematics, astrology, alchemy, and hermeticism. The personal library of Celestino, a specialist in the medieval Islamic world, comprises books written in Persian, Sanskrit, and Arabic.
Giovanni Virginio Schiaparelli, the older brother of Elsa's father, is the first astronomer to give a detailed description of the surface of Mars in Le Opere, published in 1877, in which he identifies giant rectilinear lines that might be canals. This discovery plays a key role in the creation of myths about Mars in France via Camille Flammarion's *Astronomie populaire*, (1880; English translation: *Popular Astronomy*, 1894).Her father's cousin, Ernesto Schiaparelli, is the Egyptologist who discovered the tomb of Nefertari, a queen of Egypt, in the Valley of the Queens. He is the first director of the Museo Egizio in Turin, where his discoveries are exhibited.

1911

Elsa's book of poems, *Arethusa*, is published by Quintieri in Milan.

1913

She sets out for London where she is hired as an au pair. She takes a detour to Paris. A friend of the family, the historian Alberto Lumbroso, invites her to accompany him to a costume ball given by Monsieur and Madame Henraux at their home on Rue Jasmin in the sixteenth arrondissement. Marie-Bernières-Henraux is a well-known sculptor and a former student of Rodin. For the event, Schiaparelli makes a dark blue crepe de chine dress that she wraps around her body and also wears an orange silk turban made with fabric bought at Galeries Lafayette.

1914

In London she is impressed by a lecture given by Wilhelm Wendt De Kerlor, a young Franco-Swiss theosophist. She is smitten.
July 21: They get married in a simple civil ceremony.

1915

The couple settles in Nice.

1916

The couple sets out for New York on the *Chicago*, a liner of the Compagnie Générale Transatlantique. Among the passengers is Gabriële Buffet-Picabia, wife of the Dada artist Francis Picabia.

April 20: The couple moves into the Brevoort Hotel on the corner of Fifth Avenue and Eighth Street in Manhattan.

1917

Schiaparelli meets Blanche Hays, wife of the well-known lawyer Arthur Garfield Hays, in New York.
She accompanies the Polish opera singer Ganna Walska to Cuba where she has been invited to sing Fedora. Elsa has an excellent memory of this trip and they become friends.

1918

Elsa and Wilhelm move to Boston.

1919

October 25: Death of her father in Rome.
The couple lives on Charles Street in Boston.

1920

June 15: Birth of her daughter Maria Luisa Yvonne Radha De Kerlor, nicknamed Gogo.
Her friend Gabriële Buffet-Picabia, known as Gaby, introduces her to Marcel Duchamp and Man Ray. The latter offers to photograph her in his studio.
Now separated from her unfaithful husband, she moves with her daughter to an apartment near Patchin Place in Greenwich Village.

1921

July 14: Man Ray moves to Paris.
She spends the summer in Woodstock, New York, a favorite place of the artistic community. She becomes friends with Blanche Hays, who is divorcing her husband, and Blanche persuades her to accompany her to Paris.

1922

In June, she changes the name of her daughter, who has American nationality, to Schiaparelli. Encouraged by Blanche Hays, she leaves for Paris with her daughter.
First they live at Gabriële Buffet-Picabia's home on Rue des Petits-Champs. They then stay in Blanche Hays' apartment on Boulevard de la Tour-Maubourg where Blanche, now separated from her husband, lives with her daughter Lora.
Elsa begins divorce proceedings. She hastily goes to Rome to get a new passport in her maiden name of Schiaparelli. Her mother asks her to stay and live with her, but she chooses freedom and prefers to create her own destiny. She returns to Paris and finds work, looking for objects to sell, with an antique dealer. She lives with her daughter in a small, one-bedroom apartment on Rue de l'Université.
In the summer, Blanche Hays introduces her to her friend Paul Poiret in his town house on Rue du Faubourg Saint-Honoré. She admires the designer, who then becomes her mentor and encourages her to take an interest in fashion.
She spends time with the Dadaists, especially Tristan Tzara and Francis Picabia.

1924

On December 24, she is invited by Paul Poiret to celebrate Christmas Eve in his new town house near the Rond-Point des Champs-Élysées.

1925

She is hired as a designer at Lambal, a small couture house at 11 rue du 29-Juillet in Paris founded by Madame Hartley, an American friend of Blanche Hays. Lambal closes the following year for financial reasons. This experience gives her the confidence to launch her own label.
The surrealist movement, which is revolutionizing literary and artistic life, develops in Paris.
Man Ray brings her to Le Boeuf sur le Toit, the fashionable new cabaret-bar. She meets many artists there, including Jean Cocteau.

1927

In January, she presents her first collection of handknit sweaters in her Paris apartment, 20 rue de l'Université.
In November, the American company Wm. H. Davidow Sons Co. becomes the exclusive wholesaler of Schiaparelli designs in the United States.
December 5: She joins forces with Charles Kahn and founds her company in France with a capital of 100,000 francs.
December 15: A trompe l'oeil sweater appears in American *Vogue* magazine. She opens her new couture salon, Schiaparelli – Pour le sport, at 4 rue de la Paix.

1928

May 2: Death of her husband Wilhelm De Kerlor at the age of thirty-nine in Mexico.
In November: As proof of her success, the knitting pattern for the sweater with a trompe l'oeil bow is published by *Ladies' Home Journal* magazine without mentioning Schiaparelli's name. She makes her first evening dress, a long black crepe de chine sheath dress worn under a white crepe de chine jacket. She hires the American Bettina Jones, who becomes her right-hand woman.

1929

November 18: She returns to New York for the first time on the *Berengaria*. Accompanied by Gabrielle di Robilant, her fitting model from Italy, they stay there for a month.
November 20: She shows a sportswear collection at Stewart & Co.

1930

In March, *Ladies' Home Journal* magazine publishes an article by Schiaparelli, "Smartness Aloft."
Collaborated with the milliner Madame Agnès for the spring collection.
In December, the Aspirin porcelain necklace designed for Schiaparelli by Elsa Triolet features in *Harper's Bazaar*.

1931

In June, the American Hortense MacDonald becomes the communications director at Schiaparelli, writing the texts presenting the house's fashion collections. Schiaparelli moves to a new apartment on Boulevard Saint-Germain and hires Jean-Michel Frank to decorate it. He uses furniture in ceruse oak, chairs upholstered in white and green rubber, white Tunisian rugs, and a painting by the Russian painter Pavel Tchelitchew.
For the autumn collection, she collaborates with the lacquerer Jean Dunand for a long evening dress with pleats painted in a trompe l'oeil effect.
October 17: She obtains French citizenship.

1932

In March, she opens a ready-to-wear boutique, Schiaparelli – Pour le sport, pour la ville, pour le soir, on the ground floor of her couture salon.

1933

February 23: She arrives in New York on the *Conte di Savoia*.
March 23: The company Schiaparelli Inc. is registered in the states of Delaware and New York.
In November, she opens the Schiaparelli boutique at 6 Upper Grosvenor Street in London.

1934

August 13: She appears on the cover of *Time* magazine.
She moves to a new apartment decorated by Jean-Michel Frank on Rue Barbet-de-Jouy.
She launches a fragrance collection.

1935

In January, she moves her salon from the cramped apartment on Rue de la Paix to a ninety-eight-room town house at 21 place Vendôme, previously occupied by the Chéruit couture house. She asks Jean-Michel Frank to modernize the rooms of the new salon in the building, designated a historical monument.
February 5: Presentation of the Stop, Look, and Listen collection in the new setting of her three main reception salons, all painted white. Soft light floods the space thanks to lights hidden in abstract plaster columns designed by Alberto Giacometti.
In July, she visits Vienna and travels to Hungary. She negotiates with Swarovski to use its crystal-studded fabric to make her evening capes and dresses.
In November, she is invited to participate in the first French trade fair in Moscow. She is accompanied by her communications director, Hortense MacDonald, and the British photographer Cecil Beaton.

1936

November 18: She leaves for New York on the ocean liner *Europa*.
December 28: She returns to France on the ocean liner *Normandie*.
Her first fashion collaboration with Salvador Dalí and a jewelry collaboration with Meret Oppenheim.

1937

April 29: Launch of the perfume Shocking, whose bottle is designed by Leonor Fini, and launch of the color shocking pink.
Collaboration with Jean Cocteau.
In June she opens her perfume boutique at 21 place Vendôme, designed by Jean-Michel Frank. Shaped like a gold-painted bamboo bird cage, it could hold up to eight people. Recorded song from birds on a swing hanging from the ceiling. Fragrances and cosmetic were placed on "bird-feeder" shelves. Scattered small flowers attached to the cage frame were identical to those on the stoppers of the Shocking perfume bottles.
June 19: Maison Schiaparelli has 310 employees.
She moves into her new home at 22 rue de Berri.
November 29: She leaves for New York on the ocean liner *Queen Mary*.
December 8: She returns from New York on the ocean liner *Normandie*.

1938

She transforms Les Parfums Schiaparelli into an independent company with her associate Henry S. Horn. The perfume activity moves from number 21 to number 12 place Vendôme.
Creation of an American branch of Parfums Schiaparelli whose headquarters in the Rockefeller Center were decorated by Jean-Michel Frank.
Maison Schiaparelli now has between 600 and 650 employees.

1939 She closes her London boutique at 6 Grosvenor Street.
October 31: Maison Schiaparelli has 150 employees.

1940 In January, her daughter Gogo, nicknamed Mitzi Maginot, signs up to be part of a French brigade of ambulance drivers.
July 17: She arrives in New York on the Yankee Clipper seaplane.

1941 March 4: She returns to Paris for a few months.
March 7: Gogo Schiaparelli marries Robert Lawrence Berenson, the nephew of the art historian Bernard Berenson, in New York.
May 25: She flies on the Dixie Clipper from Lisbon to New York where she stays until 1945.
During her four-year sojourn in the United States, the Place Vendôme couture salon is run by Irène Dana.

1942 In February, the Place Vendôme salon is placed under German administration.
In October, in New York, she, André Breton, and Marcel Duchamp organize the *First Papers of Surrealism* exhibition to benefit the Coordinating Council of French Relief Societies, a charity that collected funds for French prisoners of war and war orphans. The first large surrealist exhibition in the United States to the public, it runs from October 14 to November 7. André Breton designs the catalog; the cover is illustrated by Marcel Duchamp who also transformed the exhibition space using string.

1945 February 21: Maison Schiaparelli has 206 employees.
July 2: She returns to France on the luxury liner SS Mariposa.
September 13: Presentation of the first postwar Schiaparelli collection.

1946 Launch of the Le Roy Soleil perfume with a bottle, produced by Baccarat, and advertising campaign, both by Salvador Dalí.

1947 February 15: Birth of Marisa Berenson, granddaughter of Elsa Schiaparelli.
Elsa Schiaparelli asks nineteen-year-old Hubert de Givenchy to be her first assistant before naming him creative director of the boutique.

1948 April 14: Birth of Berinthia, known as Berry Berenson, granddaughter of Elsa Schiaparelli.

1949 July 28: Paris haute couture employees go on strike.
August 4: Schiaparelli presents her winter 1949–50 collection despite the strikes.
September 26: During a trip to the United States, she appears on the cover of *Newsweek* with the title "Schiaparelli the Shocker."

1950 She buys a house in Hammamet, Tunisia.

1951	Hubert de Givenchy leaves Maison Schiaparelli. Philippe Venet is named assistant designer for the salon. Schiaparelli donates an evening dress and pair of gloves from her personal wardrobe to the Metropolitan Museum of Art in New York.
1952	In January 1952, Hubert de Givenchy opens his own couture house.
1953	Philippe Venet leaves Schiaparelli to work with Hubert de Givenchy as a master tailor.
1954	In the spring, her autobiography is published simultaneously by E. P. Dutton & Co. in New York, by J. M. Dent & Sons in London, and by Denoël in Paris. February 3: Presentation of her last couture collection. December 13: The Schiaparelli salon declares bankruptcy. The perfume and license activities continue. Schiaparelli keeps her home at 22 rue de Berri.
1964	She donates seven garments to the Victoria and Albert Museum in London.
1969	She donates 43 garments and 17 accessories to the Philadelphia Museum of Art via the Fashion Group.
1971	She donates 66 garments and 22 accessories as well as 6,387 sketches to the Union Française des Arts du Costume (Ufac) in Paris.
1973	November 13: Elsa Schiaparelli dies in her sleep at home in Paris after a long illness at the age of eighty-three. She is buried in the cemetery of Frucourt, a rural town in the French department of the Somme. December 1: Masses are held for her at Saint-Philippe-du-Roule in Paris and St. Thomas More Church in New York. At the news of her death, Hubert de Givenchy declares: “Her death is a great shock. She was a fabulous woman.” Yves Saint Laurent remarks: “She was a woman whom I admired very much.”

The dates and events of this chronology are taken from the one drawn up by Dilys Blum for the catalog of the Elsa Schiaparelli exhibition at Musée de la Mode et du Textile, 2004, and from *Elsa Schiaparelli: A Biography* (London: Fig Tree, 2014).

Selected Bibliography

ADES, Dawn, Donald ALBRECHT, Pierre BERGÉ *et al.*, *Schiaparelli et les artistes*, New York, Rizzoli, 2017.

BALLARD, Bettina. *In My Fashion*. London: Secker & Warburg, 1960.

BELLOIR, Véronique. *Déboutonner la mode*. Exh. cat. Paris: Les Arts Décoratifs, 2015.

BIZOT, Chantal, Évelyne POSSÉMÉ, and Marie-Noël DE GARY. *The Jewels of Jean Schlumberger*. Translated by Alexandra Bonfante-Warren. New York: Harry N. Abrams, 2001.

BLUM, Dilys E. *Shocking! The Art and Fashion of Elsa Schiaparelli*. Exh. cat. Philadelphia: Philadelphia Museum of Art, 2003.

BONNEY, Thérèse, and Louise BONNEY. *A Shopping Guide to Paris*. New York: Robert M. McBride & Company, 1929.

CALAME-LEVERT, Florence, ed. *Les Bijoux d'Elsa Triolet. De neige et de rêve*. Paris: Le Chêne, 2015.

Dalí & Schiaparelli. Exh. cat. St. Petersburg, FL: Salvador Dalí Museum, 2017.

DALÍ, Salvador. "Objets à fonctionnement symbolique," *Le Surréalisme au service de la révolution* 3 (December 1931).

DUPLESSIS, Yves. *Le Surréalisme*. Paris: Presses universitaires de France, 1950.

Fashion Forward: 300 Years of Fashion. Exh. cat. New York: Rizzoli, 2017.

Les Folles Années de la soie. Exh. cat. Lyon: Musée Historique des Tissus, 1975.

FRYDMAN, Jaqueline. *Bodyguard : une collection privée de bijoux d'artistes*. Exh. cat. Paris: Passage de Retz, 2010.

GARLAND, Madge. *The Indecisive Decade*. London: Macdonald, 1968.

GARNIER, Guillaume. ed. *Paris couture, années trente*. Exh. cat. Paris: Musée de la Mode et du Costume, 1987.

Givenchy, 40 ans de création. Exh. cat. Paris: Paris-Musées, 1991.

GUIGON, Emmanuel. ed. *Bijoux d'artistes, une collection*. Exh. cat. Milan: Silvana Editoriale, 2012.

Hommage à Elsa Schiaparelli. Exh. cat. Paris: Musée de la Mode et du Costume, 1984.

HUGO, Pierre, Jérôme PEIGNOT, and Gaëtan PICON. *Bijoux d'artistes / Artist's Jewels, Hommage à François Hugo*. Aix-en-Provence: Les Cyprès Éditeur, 2001.

MAN RAY. *La Photographie n'est pas l'art*. Paris: GLM, 1937.

MAN RAY. *Self-Portrait*. Boston: Little, Brown and Company, 1963.
Man Ray et la Mode. Exh. cat. Paris: Rmn-Grand Palais, 2019.

MARCILHAC, Félix and Amélie MARCILHAC. *Jean Dunand*. Paris: Éditions Norma, 2020.

MAURIÈS, Patrick. *Maison Lesage: Haute Couture Embroidery*. London: Thames and Hudson, 2020.

MAURIÈS, Patrick, and Évelyne POSSÉMÉ. *Flora: The Art of Jewelry*. Translated by Ruth Sharman. London: Thames and Hudson, 2017.

MAURIÈS, Patrick, and Évelyne POSSÉMÉ. *Figures & Faces: The Art of Jewelry*. London: Thames and Hudson, 2018.

POIRET, Paul. *En habillant l'époque*. Paris: Bernard Grasset, 1930.

POIRET, Paul. *Revenez-y*, Paris: Gallimard, 1932.

PY, Françoise. "Le surréalisme et les métamorphoses : pour une mythologie moderne," *Mélusine* 26 (2006).

Schiaparelli and the Artists. New York: Rizzoli, 2017.

SCHIAPARELLI, Elsa. *Shocking*. Paris: Denoël, 1954.

SCHIAPARELLI, Elsa. *Shocking Life*. London: J. M. Dent & Sons, 1954.

SCHIAPARELLI, Elsa. *Shocking Life*. New York: E. P. Dutton & Co., 1954.

SECREST, Meryle. *Elsa Schiaparelli: A Biography*. London: Fig Tree, 2014.

SETTLE, Alison. *Clothes Line*. London: Methuen and Company, 1937.

THOMSON, Virgil. *Virgil Thomson by Virgil Thomson*. New York: Alfred A. Knopf, 1966.

WHITE, Palmer. *Elsa Schiaparelli: Empress of Paris Fashion*. London: Aurum Press, 1986.

WHITE, Palmer. *Haute Couture Embroidery: The Art of Lesage*. New York: Vendome Press, 1988.

Index

This book was published on the occasion of the exhibition Shocking: *The Surreal World of Elsa Schiaparelli* held at the Musée des Arts Décoratifs, Paris, July 6, 2022–January 22, 2023.

Exhibition conceived by Les Arts Décoratifs, Paris, produced with the support of Maison Schiaparelli

Schiaparelli

Restoration of the Musée des Arts Décoratifs' Schiaparelli ensembles:
Support is provided by Marina Kellen French and The Anna-Maria & Stephen Kellen Foundation

EXHIBITION

Chief Curator

Olivier Gabet

Curator

Marie-Sophie Carron de la Carrière
Chief Curator, Musée des Arts Décoratifs, fashion and textile department

Assisted by
Marie-Pierre Ribère
Assistant Curator, Musée des Arts Décoratifs, fashion and textile department

Production

Stéphane Perl
Head of Production

Sarah Ben Hamida
Charlotte Frelat
Production and Project Management

Exhibition Design

Agence NC
Nathalie Crinière
Maëlys Chevillot

Signage
Anamorphée
Bertrand Houdin
Théo Garnier-Greuez
Giovanna Caliari

CATALOG

Head of Publications and Images Department
Chloé Demey

Editorial and Picture Research Coordinator
Violaine Aurias

Translation
Carol Lipton
Chrisoula Petridis
Kate Robinson

Copyediting
Chrisoula Petridis

Graphic design
Anamorphée
Bertrand Houdin
Giovanna Caliari
Théo Garnier-Greuez

Photoengraving
Fotimprim, Paris

The Authors

Dilys Blum
The Jack M. and Annette Y. Friedland Senior Curator of Costume and Textiles, Philadelphia Museum of Art

Marie-Sophie Carron de la Carrière
Chief Curator, Musée des Arts Décoratifs, fashion and textile department

Emmanuelle de l'Écotais
Historian of photography, Man Ray specialist, former head of the photographic collections, Musée d'Art Moderne de Paris

Jean-Louis Gaillemin
Art historian, critic, curator

Patrick Mauriès
Writer and publisher

Maire-Pierre Ribère
Assistant Curator, Musée des Arts Décoratifs, fashion and textile department

Hanya Yanagihara
She is the author of three novels, including *To Paradise*. She lives in New York

ACKNOWLEDGMENTS

The Musée des Arts Décoratifs would like to sincerely thank Maison Schiaparelli for its support and generosity, particularly
The Della Valle family, Owner
Delphine Bellini, Chief Executive Officer
Daniel Roseberry, Art Director
Tim Watson, Creative Coordinator
Francesco Pastore, Head of Heritage and Cultural Projects

We are indebted to the institutions and collectors who have made this exhibition possible thanks to their generous loans:

Antwerp

Collection Sylvio Perlstein

Berlin

Deutsche Kinemathek
Florian Bolenius
Barbara Schröter
Andrea Ziegenbruch

Chichester

West Dean College of Arts and Conservation
Frances Norris
Sarah Hughes
Hugh Morrison

Figueres

Fundació Gala-Salvador Dalí
Montse Aguer
Rosa Aguer
Irene Civil
Bea Crespo

London

Victoria and Albert Museum
Tristram Hunt
Liz Wilkinson

Marseille

Musée Cantini
Claude Miglietti
Guillaume Theulière

Monaco

Collection Edmond Henrard
Edmond Henrard
Éric Blanchegorge

Nantes

Musée d'Arts de Nantes
Sophie Lévy
Céline Rincé-Vaslin

New York

The Metropolitan Museum of Art
Max Hollein
Andrew Bolton
Emily Foss
Elizabeth Schaeffer
Anne Yanofsky

The Museum of Modern Art
Glenn D. Lowry
Clément Chéroux
Carla Caputo
Tasha Lutek

The New York Public Library
Tony Marx
Deborah Straussman

Mark Walsh Collection
Mark Walsh

Paris

Bibliothèque Historique de la Ville de Paris
Emmanuelle Toulet
Bérengère de l'Épine
Caroline Lahaye

Bibliothèque Nationale de France
Laurence Engel
Sylvie Ferreira

Centre des Monuments Nationaux
Philippe Bélaval
Laurent Bergeot
Isabelle Grasswill

Christie's
Cécile Verdier
Alixe du Cluzeau

Fondation Azzedine Alaïa
Carla Sozzani
Olivier Saillard
Sandrine Tinturier

Galerie Minsky
Arlette Souhami

Maison Schiaparelli
Delphine Bellini
Daniel Roseberry
Timothy Watson
Francesco Pastore

Musée National d'Art Moderne – Centre Pompidou
Laurent Le Bon
Xavier Rey
Nicolas Liucci-Goutnikov
Manon Sarda
Raphaële Bianchi
Mariolina Cilurzo
Laurianne Nehlig
Nathalie Cissé-Mongaillard
Robin Lety

Musée Picasso
Cécile Debray
Marie Liard-Dexet

Musée de l'Orangerie
Christophe Leribault
Claire Bernardi
Thomas Eschbach
Alice Marsal

Musée Yves Saint Laurent
Madison Cox
Aurélie Samuel
Judith Lamas
Tiphaine Musset
Amandine Périnel

Palais Galliera
Miren Arzalluz
Marie-Ange Bernieri
Corinne Dom
Hélène Favrel
Sylvie Lécallier
Sophie Grossiord
Marie-Laure Gutton

Secret Gallery
Nathalie Elmaleh
Laurent Teboul

Philadelphia

Philadelphia Museum of Art
Timothy Rub
Dilys Blum
Hannah Kauffman
Berenice Morris
Sara Reiter

Reading, Pennsylvania

Gene London Cinema Collection
John D. Thomas

Saint-Étienne Métropole

Musée d'Art Moderne et Contemporain
Aurélie Voltz
Alexandre Quoi
Évelyne Granger
Florent Molle

Saint-Étienne-du-Rouvray

Bibliothèque Elsa Triolet
Édouard Benard
Martine Thomas

Saint-Ouen

Falbalas
Françoise de Fligué

Scottsdale, Arizona

Susan Casden Collection
Susan Casden

St. Petersburg, Florida

Dalí Museum
Hank Hine
William Jeffett
Allison McCarthy
Shaina Buckles Harkness

Versailles

Château de Versailles
Catherine Pégard
Laurent Salomé
Marie-Laure de Rochebrune
Frédéric Lacaille
Morgane Bertho

as well as those who have preferred to remain anonymous.

We are grateful to all those who have contributed to the preparation of the exhibition and the accompanying catalog:
Valérie Belin, Anaïs David, Christophe Dellière, Pascal Brunel, Diktats bookshop (Monsieur Antoine and Monsieur Nicolas), Karin Kato, Nicolas Polowski, Marco de Rivera, Benjamin Roi.

And finally, at the Musée des Arts Décoratifs, our warmest thanks to:

the conservation department, particularly Sonia Aubès, Romain Condamine, Louise Curtis, Christelle Di Giovanni, Anne Forray-Carlier, Dominique Forest, Bénédicte Gady, Amélie Gastaut, Audrey Gay-Mazuel, Catherine Gouédo, Astrid Grange, Pauline Juppin, Karine Lacquemant, Sophie Motsch, Marion Neveu, Joffrey Picq, Cloé Pitiot, Évelyne Possémé, Éric Pujalet-Plaà, Hélène Renaudin, and Sébastien Quéquet; as well as Guillaume del Rio and Killian Petit;

the collection department, particularly Florence Bertin, Maxime Blanckaert, Ségolène Bonnet, Catherine Didelot, Valentine Dubard, Emmanuelle Garcin, Valérie Graslin, Cécile Huguet-Broquet, Aude Mansouri, Alexandra Mérieux, Estelle Savoye, Myriam Tessier, and Luna Violante; as well as Bathilde Grenier, Hoa Perriguey, Anne-Gaëlle Dufour, Romane Dupont, and Stéphanie Wahli;

the library and documentation department, particularly Emmanuelle Beuvin, Laure Haberschill, and Marie Wattier;

the production and international development department, particularly Auriabelle Grimaud and Agathe Mercier;

the communications department, particularly Anne-Solène Delfolie and Isabelle Mendoza;

the publications and images department, particularly Aurélien Locatelli and Marion Servant;

the sponsorship and privatization department, particularly Nathalie Coulon, Mélite de Foucaud, and Nina Vigneron;

the administrative and financial department, particularly Viviane Besombes, Valérie Fauvel and Nour Mouhaidine;

the museum administration, particularly Liliia Polshcha.

COPYRIGHT

PHOTOGRAPHIC CREDITS

Cover:
PHOEBUS EVENING CAPE
Winter 1938–39
Ratteen, quilted silk crepe, paillette, tinsel, and gold thread embroidery by Lesage, passementerie buttons
Musée des Arts Décoratifs, Paris. Gift of Elsa Schiaparelli, Ufac, 1973
Inv. UF 73-21-39
Photo : © Les Arts Décoratifs/ Valérie Belin

pp. 13–16, 38, 43, 50, 53, 60, 63, 77, 80 (t), 81, 85, 89, 92, 93 (except bl), 100 (t), 104, 108, 109 (t), 112 (tr), 113, 117, 121, 125 (t), 128 (t), 129, 133, 136 (b), 137, 141, 145, 153 (t), 161 (b), 169, 172, 176, 181, 185, 188, 192 (t), 193, 197, 206 (16): © Les Arts Décoratifs / Christophe Dellière
p. 23: Maison Schiaparelli
p. 24: University of California Collection
pp. 26, 31, 47, 55, 59, 84 (t): Philadelphia Museum of Art
p. 27: © Hulton Archives / Getty Images
pp. 33, 35, 39: © Centre Pompidou, MNAM-CCI, Dist. RMN-Grand Palais / image Centre Pompidou, MNAM-CCI
p. 36: © Don Ross
pp. 37, 40: © Bibliothèque nationale de France
pp. 46, 96 (t): © The Metropolitan Museum of Art, Dist. RMN-Grand Palais / image MMA
pp. 48, 51, 56 (b), 58, 61, 80b, 88b, 93bg, 100b, 105b, 112hg, 120b, 125b, 128b, 132, 140 (t), 153b, 156, 161 (t), 164 (t), 168, 173 (t), 177 (t), 180 (t), 184 (t), 189b, 192b, 196, 212–43: © Les Arts Décoratifs
p. 56 (t): West Dean College of Arts and Conservation
p. 64 (g): © GRANGER / Alamy Stock Photo
pp. 71, 75, 79, 83, 87, 91, 95, 99, 103, 107, 111, 115, 119, 123, 127, 131, 135, 139, 143, 147, 151, 155, 159, 163, 167, 171, 175, 179, 183, 187, 191, 195: © Les Arts Décoratifs / Valérie Belin
p. 72 (t): Photography Collection, The New York Public Library
pp. 73, 101, 116 (except tl), 120h, 124, 149, 152, 157, 160, 165, 202 (7), 203 (8), 204–05, 207: © Les Arts Décoratifs / Jean Tholance
p. 76: © Paris Musées, Palais Galliera, Dist. RMN-Grand Palais / image ville de Paris
p. 84 (b): © Centre Pompidou, MNAM-CCI, Dist. RMN-Grand Palais / Guy Carrard
p. 96 (b): © The LIFE Picture Collection/Shutterstock
p. 105 (t): Collection Kharbine-Tapabor
p. 109 (b): © Roger-Viollet
p. 132: © Château de Versailles, Dist. RMN-Grand Palais / Christophe Fouin
p. 148: © Illustrated London News/Mary Evans Picture Library
p. 173 (b): Thierry Coudert, *Café Society*, p. 28
p. 177 (b): Universal photo/ Sipa
p. 180 (b): Bettmann / Bettmann / *via* Getty Images
p. 184 (b): Lido/Sipa
p. 189 (t), 202 (2): © Maison Schiaparelli
pp. 246–57: Courtesy Maison Schiaparelli
pp. 261–75: © Les Arts Décoratifs / Christophe Dellière and Jean Tholance

First published in the United Kingdom in 2022 by Thames & Hudson Ltd, 181A High Holborn, London WC1V 7QX

First published in the United States of America in 2022 by Thames & Hudson Inc., 500 Fifth Avenue, New York, New York 10110

British Library Cataloguing-in-Publication Data
A catalogue record for this book is available from the British Library

Library of Congress Control 2022937031

ISBN 978-0-500-02594-9

Printed and bound in Italy